The Cypress Hills

The Cypress Hills

AN ISLAND BY ITSELF

Walter Hildebrandt

&

Brian Hubner

PURICH
PUBLISHING
LIMITED
SASKATOON, SK. CANADA

Purich Publishing Ltd.
Box 23032, Market Mall Post Office, Saskatoon, SK, Canada, S7J 5H3
Phone: (306) 373-5311 Fax: (306) 373-5315 Email: purich@sasktel.net
Website: www.purichpublishing.com

Library and Archives Canada Cataloguing in Publication

Hildebrandt, Walter
    The Cypress Hills : an island by itself / Walter Hildebrandt & Brian Hubner. — New ed.

Includes bibliographical references and index.
ISBN 978-1-895830-30-9

    1. Cypress Hills (Alta. and Sask.) — History. 2. Métis — Cypress Hills (Alta. and Sask.) — History. 3. Indians of North America — Cypress Hills (Alta. and Sask.) — History. 4. Métis — Government relations. 5. Indians of North America — Canada — Government relations. I. Hubner, Brian, 1958– II. Title

FC3545.C96H55 2007   971.24'3   C2007-902807-1

Cover design by Duncan Campbell.
Cover photo: Adams Lake in the Cypress Hills, by Robin Karpan.
Editing, design, and layout by Donald Ward.
Index by Ursula Acton.
Maps by William Mills.
Printed and bound in Canada by Houghton Boston Printers & Lithographers, Saskatoon

The publishers gratefully acknowledge the assistance of the Government of Canada through the Book Publishing Industry Development Program and the Government of Saskatchewan through the Cultural Industries Development Fund for its publishing program.

This book is printed on 100 per cent post-consumer
recycled and ancient-forest-friendly paper.

FORT WALSH HAS BEEN DISMANTLED and the police station moved to Maple Creek. Very likely at some future day admirers of ancient ruins will re-discover its desolate mud chimneys and entwine them with romances such as the poetry loving people of the east believe to be the lot of every man who preceded the CPR. And possibly some policeman of "ye olden time," then a portly rancher or business man, with a double chin and a half dozen children, will visit the scene and, forgetting that the lot of a policeman is not a happy one, will chase his buffalo and fight his battles over again, telling of adventures in the imminent breach, of hair breadth escapes by flood and field, of balls in which the barracks were graced by the youth and beauty from all the neighbouring reserves, and altogether drawing the long bow with such a vengeance that the mud chimneys will wink at each other and grin horribly a ghastly smile.

Edmonton Bulletin
August 18, 1883

CONTENTS

ACKNOWLEDGEMENTS

THIS BOOK IS BASED ON RESEARCH I did for the Canadian Parks Service while working as an historian responsible for the history of Fort Walsh National Historic Site. I have rewritten and reshaped material that originally served program needs and was used by the guides interpreting the history of the Cypress Hills to the public at the fort and at Farwell's Trading Post.

Brian Hubner made valuable contributions both in research and writing. I met Brian as an enthusiastic guide some years ago. His dedicated search for material in repositories throughout Canada and the United States — particularly his interviews with ancestors of those who once lived and worked in the Cypress Hills — added greatly to this book.

I would like to thank the many colleagues I worked with during my years at the Canadian Parks Service from 1978 to 1992 — the historians, archaeologists, planners, engineers, architects, interpreters, and administrators.

Over the years — once, sometimes twice a year — I would travel to the Cypress Hills to talk to the guides about the history of the site. I thank the guides I spoke with as we discussed an imbalance in the historical record that favoured settler society and gave little space to the perspective of the Aboriginal people who lived in the Cypress Hills. Together, we began a process of inclusion that we must continue.

In the summer of 2005 I travelled to Carry the Kettle Reserve to read the Nakoda chapter to elders and others who were interested. I would like to thank the various people in the different locations for their comments and for the often fascinating discussion. I would like to thank especially Val Rider and Elsie Koochicum for facilitating my visit, and for their comments as well.

Thanks to the following Elders and members of Carry the Kettle band, both for written material and oral history that contributed to the writing of the Nakoda chapter: Tony Ashdohonk, Angeline Eashappie, Elmer Eashappie, Georgina Eashappie, Ida Eashappie, Madeline Eashappie, Nancy Eashappie, Sarah Eashappie, Sadie Haywahe, Wilfred Haywahe, Marita Hotomani, Alice Ironstar, Pearl Jack, Kenneth Kennedy, Wilma Kennedy, Alice Lavallee, Bertha O'Watch, Jerry Prettysheild, Wanda Prettysheild, Percy Rider, Vincent Rider, Gertude Rope, Delmar Runns, Larry Runns, Andrew Ryder, Rena Ryder, Aletha Saulteaux, Bernice Saulteaux, Mary Scribe, Edna Spencer, Lloyd Thompson, William (Billy) Thompson, Beverly Thomson, Cecil Thomson, Cora Thomson, Nelson Thomson, Phyllis Thomson, Shirley Thomson,

William S. Thomson, Herb Walker, Arlette Whitecap, Floyd Whitecap; and the late Alex Ashdohonk, Jerome Ashdohonk, Violet Ashdohonk, Lena Eashappie, Levi Eashappie, Cora Grey, William Grey, John Haywahe, Wallace Haywahe, Henry Ironstar, Amy Kakakaway, Eva Lapierre, Paul Leader, Steve Moonface, Velma O'Watch, Isabelle Prettysheild, Leslie Prettysheild, Alma Rider, George Rider, Ernest Rope, Claudia Runns, Earl Runns, Lucy Ryder, Sarah Ryder, Dr. Jesse Saulteaux, Elizabeth Thompson, Kaye Thompson, Lawrence Thompson, Urban Thompson, and Kenneth Thomson.

For transcripts of the stories and memories of the late Elders I am indebted to Albert Eashappie, Jim Ryder, and Maggie Jack Walker. I am also indebted to Carry the Kettle council members: Chief James O'Watch, Arthur Adams, Joel Ashdohonk, Joyce Ironstar, Bernard Jack, and Howard Thomson. Staff assisting the Elders included Marie Eashappie, Judy Grey, Kathy Jack, Karen Spencer, and Kelly Thomson. Co-ordinators were Elsie Jack-Koochicum and Valerie Rider. To all, my grateful thanks.

I dedicate this book to the guides at Fort Walsh, and especially to Sarah, who was one of them.

Walter Hildebrandt
April 2007

FIRSTLY, I WOULD LIKE ACKNOWLEDGE the contributions of my mother, Freda, who sadly passed away in 2005, for typing the first edition of this book. Secondly, I would like to thank my father, Ed, who first instilled in me a love of the history of the West, who travelled with me on many of my research trips to Montana, and who assisted with selling copies of the first edition. Thirdly, I would like to thank my wife, Eileen, for her assistance with typing the second edition and her careful proofreading, and for her encouragement with writing both editions of the book.

Finally, I would like to dedicate this book to Eileen, and to our children, Xavier and Cedric; may we make many more trips, together, to the Cypress Hills.

Brian Hubner
April 2007

BOTH AUTHORS WOULD LIKE TO THANK those who assisted in the research for this book. In a project that stretched over a decade there were many archivists and librarians who were helpful in gathering photographs, books, and documents. Three descendants of the Cypress Hills traders were generous in sharing their personal records, photographs, and memories: George C. Lande of Pryor, Montana, a great-grandson of Abel Farwell; Leonard J. Hammond of Deer Lodge, Montana, grandson of George L. Hammond and Rosalie Wills; and Winniefred Eastlund Arhelger, great-granddaughter of Moses Solomon.

Thanks to the staff at the Glenbow Museum, the Saskatchewan Archives Board, the Adam Shortt Library of Canadiana (University of Saskatchewan), Library and Archives Canada, the Archives of Manitoba, the University of Manitoba Archives & Special Collections, the Provincial Archives of Alberta, the Fort Assiniboine Preservation Association, the William K. Kohrs Memorial Library, the Historical Society of Minnesota, and the Montana Historical Society. Thanks to Bill Mills for drawing the maps, and to George Melnyk, Jane McHughen, and Donald Ward for editing. Also, special thanks to Joel Overholser, Donny White, Margaret Anne Kennedy, Lianne Roberts, Mimi Martin, Tom Kynman, Richard Stuart, Julie Stafford, Chris Kotecki, and Sherry Farrell Racette.

Foreword to the New Edition

I AM HONOURED TO BE ASKED to follow in the footsteps of the late Gordon Oakes of the Nekaneet people, who wrote the foreword to the first edition of this book. When I first came to southwest Saskatchewan to live, around 1975, I could find no written, formal history of the area and its people. The first historical account that I was able to find, and it is very brief and not in much depth, was that included in the non-fiction work of the celebrated American writer and conservationist, and long-ago resident of this area, Wallace Stegner (1919-1993), called *Wolf Willow: A History, A Story, and a Memory of the Last Plains Frontier* (1962). In order to write it, Stegner must have had to go to primary sources, and, as such, his work was invaluable to anyone interested in the nearly forgotten, or disregarded, past of this fascinating area. Eventually, I found Dr. John Bennett's longitudinal study, *Northern Plainsmen*, in which he called Maple Creek "Jasper," but this was mostly a sociological work, and, living as I was in the middle of his sociology, although I was certainly interested, his book didn't add much to my scant store of knowledge about the past.

When I began seriously to wonder about history in the place in which I now made my home — partly because I couldn't answer the question as to why it was that, although the prairie that I walked showed me every day that this had been Indian land, I saw not a single First Nations face on the streets of the nearby town, and partly because I was beginning to write novels and short stories about my new home — I had finally to go to the academic literature in hopes of finding answers. If, the day I came across Professor John Tobias's paper explaining the above question, "Canada's Subjugation of the Plains Cree, 1879-1885," I felt horror at the paper's content, I was also very glad to know something solid and real about this place at last. But, of course, inevitably, Tobias's paper led me to wonder about the archaeology of the area, about the first inhabitants and their movements and their stories, a history that was simply not available to me.

With such a background of searching and mostly failing to find answers to my serious questions about the past of the place I called home, you can see why I was made very happy by the 1994 publication of the first edition of *The Cypress Hills*, with its authoritative tracing of the people of the region, its map-making of a history unseen and unknown to most of us. This new edition goes even further, including a chapter on the Nakoda people, not present in the older edition, and filling in a serious gap in our understanding of our past.

At last, now, there is a true, fairly comprehensive history for us to read. Not only scholars will be grateful, but also all of us who have made our lives here, either in the Cypress Hills as the Cree and Nakoda still do, or in the hills' shadow, as many others of us, chiefly Euro-Canadians, have from the 1880s to the present day. All of us owe a debt of gratitude to Walter Hildebrandt and Brian Hubner for undertaking this work, and to Purich Publishing for making it available to every one of us in a form that is accessible and affordable.

Sharon Butala
March 14, 2007

The Thunder Breeding Hills

THE CANADIAN WEST was never a frontier waiting to be taken or conquered. For hundreds of years the Cypress Hills were a place of rich and varied flora and fauna that the Aboriginal peoples of the prairies relied on for their subsistence. They were a place of shelter where bands wintered as they moved off the open plains to avoid the biting western winds. The game in the Hills was plentiful in both summer and winter. In the forests of the Cypress Hills grew the long and narrow lodgepole pine so prized by all the Aboriginal peoples with access to the Hills. The poles manufactured from these trees were ideal for lodge poles and for both dog and horse travois.

For some of the Aboriginal peoples, this land — which had been by-passed by the glaciers that leveled the surrounding plains — was believed to be the place where the weather came from: "The Thunder Breeding Hills." Many plains people made their way to the Hills for food and shelter, and because they were believed to be a great spiritual place. The young came for vision quests to this strange outlier, climbing to the top of hills surrounded by deep forests with grand, awesome panoramas extending far out onto the prairies.

In the nineteenth century the Métis established wintering bases in the Hills. From the shelter of the Hills they pursued the diminishing buffalo herds that rarely came into Canadian territory after the 1870s. But the role of the Métis was still important — these Métis provisioners manufactured pemmican for the fur-trade posts in Western Canada. The Métis were followed by American free traders let loose into "Whoop-Up Country" to ply their whiskey trade across the western plains in the aftermath of their Civil War. These traders, who helped with the slaughter of the buffalo, were followed by Canada's Mounties, who came to make the West safe for the white settlers who would arrive in the wake of the Cypress Hills Massacre of 1873. Thus, these mysterious and strange hills have had a long human history.

Traces of human life go back to artifacts over 8,000 years old and culminate in the cattle trails of the ranch country that makes up the most recent past. The process of history has left the hills strewn with artifacts of both humankind and nature: rock piles, bones, trails, burial sites, cellars, and fences. The Hills have been part of the full cycle of invasion, conquest, colonization, exploitation, development, and expansion that characterizes the market economies that dominate the world today.

This book is a record of the process of history, not its evolution. What has taken place in the Cypress Hills is not necessarily a progression of history; perhaps in our times we are witnessing more of a cycle of history than a linear advance. As agriculture declines on the prairies, the grasslands may once again return and along with them the buffalo. And perhaps even the grizzlies will once again return to the Hills to haunt those who, according to Isaac Cowie, killed 750 of them during one season in the days of Whoop-Up Country. They can return and join the deer, elk, antelope, and foxes that are still there.

CHAPTER ONE

The Cypress Hills and Their People

The Hills

The Cypress Hills are a flat-topped plateau covering an area of about 2,600 square kilometres in southwestern Saskatchewan and southeastern Alberta. Glaciation bulldozed the surrounding terrain, with the ice mass splitting around the Hills and leaving them intact. They are a small remnant of a large plateau that existed in the region forty million years ago, but which was later almost totally eroded. This finger of land, exposed above the glacier ice, may have been exploited by Pleistocene hunters as early as 15,000 years ago.

In more recent times, Native groups occupied the Hills seasonally as part of an annual movement to their hunting grounds out on the open plains in summer and to the shelter of hill country in winter. The Cypress Hills also contained an important resource for the Aboriginal peoples: the lodgepole pine. When the glaciers retreated from the plains, these trees survived as a key feature of this ecosystem, which is unique to the prairies. The only other environment where such pines can be found is in the Rocky Mountains. The Aboriginal peoples of the plains fashioned the poles for their lodges from the larger trees and used the smaller ones as the framework for dog and horse travois.

The Cypress Hills lie at the northern extension of an escarpment known as the Missouri Coteau. This escarpment stretches from the Souris River in the southeast, across the province of Saskatchewan and into Alberta. North and east of the escarpment lie the prairies — a rich grassland plain situated on a lowland glacial lake basin. To the northwest lie the Great Sand Hills of

Saskatchewan, a vast desert area, the remains of a glacial lake. To the south of the Cypress Hills, the terrain is gently rolling to strongly rolling hills. This topography was created by the ground moraine left by glaciation some 20,000 years ago.

The climate of the Cypress Hills area is one of extremes, fluctuating greatly from summer to winter. Summer temperatures may rise as high as 38° Celsius, with winter as low as -45°. The precipitation in the area is generally low. The average rainfall is about thirty-six centimeters, and most of this falls in June. Often, heavy rains cause rain-washing of the slopes in the coteau areas. The prevailing winds are from the west: warm, dry chinook winds often come from the west and southwest, while colder winter winds come from the northwest.

The vegetation of southwestern Saskatchewan is grassland; some undisturbed grassland habitat can still be found at Grasslands National Park just to the east of the Cypress Hills. Wild rose bushes and chokecherries grow on the hill slopes and can appear as thick growth along valley or coulee bottoms. To the northeast of the Missouri Coteau escarpment, the land is covered by mixed-grass prairies dotted with poplar. To the southwest are the short-grass plains that typically are characterized by the growth of sagebrush, with tree growth restricted to coulees and creek beds. According to geographers, the vegetation and climate have remained relatively unchanged over the past 2,000 years.

The diverse habitat of the Cypress Hills has been able to support a large number of animals and birds. Before people arrived in large numbers during the nineteenth century, when the buffalo were still plentiful on the prairies, predators such as grizzly bears, mountain lions, and wolves could be found in the Hills. Today, mostly smaller animals such as lynx, bobcat, coyote, and fox remain, although frequently big game such as elk, moose, mule deer, and white-tailed deer can be spotted. The pronghorn antelope can also still be seen in the area, especially in the grassy meadows found in the gaps between the Hills. A variety of squirrels, the striped skunk, and badger inhabit this environment as well. The aspen woodlands provide refuge for the porcupine, raccoon, and chipmunk. Along the coulees of the Hills one is most likely to find Nuttal's Cottontail and the snowshoe hare. Muskrat, mink, beaver, and a variety of weasels reside along the creeks and lakes of the Cypress Hills.

A great variety of birds can be found in the Hills — up to 207 species have been spotted. Of particular interest are the Audubon Warbler, Oregon Junco, and McGillivary's Warbler. The Hills are the breeding grounds for the Yellow-shafted Flicker and the Western Red-shafted Flicker. The larger trumpeter swan, cormorants, and Canada geese also breed in the Hills. Woodpeckers, ducks, robins, owls, buntings, swallows, bluebirds, loons, herons, hawks, eagles, and gulls are among some of the species that can still be found here.

The People

Scholars suggest that the first people crossed into North America over a land bridge into unglaciated regions of Alaska and the Yukon approximately 100,000 to 10,000 BCE (Before the Common Era). These big-game hunters from Asia pursued their game using stone-tool technology consisting of bifacial flaked knives and spear tips, as well as some microblades (thin, razor-sharp flakes of stone). As environmental conditions in the north deteriorated, these hunters migrated from the Alaska/Yukon region farther south through a corridor between two large ice sheets — the receding Laurentide to the east and the Cordilleran to the west. They moved down through this passageway into the centre of the New World. By this time a new technology was evident, described by archaeologists as Fluted Point culture because of the style of arrowheads they used for hunting. The earliest use of the Cypress Hills environment might well have been in the era between 10,000 and 8,000 BCE.

The Fluted Point people survived by hunting big game such as mammoth, mastodon, and bison, as well as smaller animals such as camel, horse, sloth, caribou, and beaver. Evidence of these prehistoric mammals has been uncovered at the east end of the Hills around the present-day community of Eastend, Saskatchewan. The Fluted Point people's clothing was made of hide and fur; their tools were made of bone and stone. Evidence of these early peoples has been found across southern parts of Canada, throughout the United States, and also in South America. Sites in northwestern Canada are limited.

The Fluted Point people were followed by the Plano people (8,000 – 4,000 BCE), who were also big-game hunters. The Plano people expanded and refined earlier stone technology: new, distinctive flaking styles emerged, as did a greater variety of hunting tools. New tools such as stone hammers are found at Plano sites, as well as the earliest evidence of cremation burials. Sites of Plano peoples are found throughout the plains area. In the northern plains area they are thought to have hunted caribou, lived in family-sized tents, and to have created a stone technology unique to the plains. As the ice retreated, the Plano peoples moved eastward to the shores of the receding waters. Evidence of their habitation in Canada has been found as far east as the St. Lawrence River and the Maritimes.

Approximately 6,000 BCE, the Early Plains people migrated northward from what is now the southern United States into Canada and onto the plains, bringing with them a new variety of notched projectile points and new hunting techniques. Coincident with the arrival of these new peoples was the arrival of a new dry climate (7,500 – 2,000 BCE). The environment was so hot that much of the archaeological record has been obliterated, making identification of materials other than stone problematic. Following the Early Plains people were the Middle Plains people (4,000 BCE to 500 CE), a predominantly bison culture.

New archaeological work undertaken in 2000-05 by Gerald Oetelaar and a team from the University of Calgary has shed new light on this period in the Cypress Hills. At the "Stampede Site," excavated six metres deep just outside of Elkwater, Alberta, artifacts were discovered from starting around 6,000 BCE or earlier, including a continuous sequence of fire pits and household debris, indicating unbroken occupation for 8,000 or 9,000 years. The site

THE EXCAVATION AT ELKWATER, ALBERTA. *The original dig at the Stampede Site, which was directed by Eugene Gryba, started in 1971 and lasted two seasons (summer 1971-72). Oetelaar's excavations at the site started in May 2000 and lasted until the summer of 2004. During the summer of 2005, they removed sediment peels from the walls of the excavations, and these were mounted in the new Interpretive Centre in Elkwater, Alberta, in January 2007* (photo courtesy Gerald A. Oetelaar).

has yielded almost a million artifacts, including finely-made scrapers, bone beads, shell beads, awls, and projectile points such as one made of white cert dating from about 4,000 BCE. Despite the torrid hot spell, volcanic ash, and floods, people always came back to the refuge that was the Hills — perhaps, it is speculated, because the area remained more stable ecologically and an oasis for wildlife such as bison. It was at this time that the cyclic use of the Cypress Hills by people such as the Blackfoot may have begun.[1]

Within Fort Walsh National Historic Site, another site was found during the rebuilding of the fort's palisade. This site has been dated to 1,200 BCE and to as early as 2,160 BCE, placing it in the Middle Plains period.

Bison herds were now the staple that provided raw material for food, shelter, and clothing. A complex social organization emerged from a people that needed to operate in large numbers in order to hunt successfully and process the buffalo. Bison herds were stampeded over cliffs or driven into pounds, ravines, or swales to be slaughtered, and the carcasses were processed into the products required by the people. Some of the many tipi rings found throughout the Cypress Hills are from this early era. There is evidence that these bison hunters lived in tents that required stone weights to secure their sides at the circumference. These stones, when rolled away, were lasting markers of their presence. The remains of deformed dog hipbones are indications that the Middle Plains people used travois pulled by dogs. Evidence of burial sites with artifacts such as stone tools, eagle talons, copper from Lake Superior, and shell beads from Atlantic areas provide clues not only to their makers' belief systems but to their trade systems as well.

Pottery finds indicate a close trading relationship between plains people and those just south of them. Also, contact with forest people to the east and northeast is evident through the gradual emergence on the plains of the Siouan-speaking Nakoda to the east and Algonquian speakers to the northwest. From the north, came the Athapaskan-speaking Beaver, Sekani, and Sarcee (Tsuu T'ina) people, the latter eventually settling in southern Alberta. From the west and south came the Algonquian-speaking Blackfoot (Siksika) and Gros Ventre (Atsina) peoples, while from the southwest came the Kootenai-

---

LEFT: *6,000-year-old artifacts from the archaeological dig at Elkwater. The item on the left is a bone awl, a tool that was used to punch holes in leather. The next item in the top row is a projectile point from an atlatl dart, a unique weapon designed to artificially lengthen the arm of the hunter, thus allowing him to propel the spear much further. The item at centre top is a piece of flaked stone which appears to have been used for cutting, and can thus be identified as a knife blade. The fourth item in this row is a large flake or chip which has been worked along the left margin. Archaeologists call these edge-modified flakes, and they are also used for cutting. The item at the extreme right is a bird bone which has been cut along the lower margin; the method is known as the groove-and-snap technique, in which the craftsperson incises a groove around the bone and then snaps off the end. One such groove is visible near the lower margin. The small rings of bone snapped off the end could then be converted into beads. The white item in the second row is a biface fragment, meaning that it is flaked on both surfaces, which could be used for a variety of cutting or scraping tasks. These artifacts come from Paleosol 10, a buried soil located about 1.5 metres below the surface which has been radiocarbon dated at 6,110 (plus or minus 90) years before the present.* (Photo courtesy of Gerald A. Oetelaar).

speaking peoples. Members of the Blackfoot Confederacy included the Siksika, the Peigans, and the Blood (Kainah).

The era from 500 CE (Common Era) to approximately 1700, or in the time of direct European contact, was characterized by the culture of the buffalo-hunting peoples who then occupied the prairies. They were influenced by the Spanish far to the south, whose horses were being traded onto the plains by the seventeenth century. There was also significant influence felt from the Missouri Valley, and for a period of time an agricultural settlement was established in southern Alberta that was an offshoot of the southern Missouri culture. Also, slowly moving to the north from Mexico and Central America through various trade networks were corn, squash, beans, sunflowers, and tobacco, and these plants began to be cultivated in parts of the southern plains.

The prairies were peopled by a variety of First Nations by 1700. The Prairie or Plains Cree occupied the eastern and central areas. The Dakota and Nakoda (Assiniboine or Stoney) were to the south of the Cree, while the Gros Ventre and the Blackfoot lived on the western extremity. The Plains Ojibwa or Saulteaux (Annishnawbe) lived to the east, with the Crow to the south of the Nakoda.

LODGEPOLE PINES. *An important resource for the peoples of the plains, these trees were used in the construction of tipis and for horse and dog travois* (photo by Robin Karpan).

The Cree, who dominated the central plains by the nineteenth century, were originally located in woodland areas to the west and north of the Great Lakes. They were a band society in which the ultimate unit of organization was the family. In small groups, they moved over their territory in search of game or to collect other food. Each family unit had an appointed leader. A number of bands could come together at various seasons, but this was rare and such groupings lasted for only short periods of time. There was no single chief for these bands and, consequently, there was little sense of unity among them. They had no controlling governing authority, but they did share a common language and had similar customs, and their social behaviour and laws were determined by public opinion. The scarcity of fish and game in woodland areas made larger gatherings impossible. Unable to come together in great numbers, they rarely went to war with neighbouring tribes; scattered in small groups in the woods, they were a difficult target for an enemy to attack.

In contrast with the family-centred Cree, traditional plains tribal societies such as that of the Blackfoot had much larger units that stayed together for longer periods of time. On the open plains it was difficult to hide from neighbouring tribes, making tribal cohesiveness a necessity for self-defence and creating more opportunities for military conflict than in the heavily treed woodlands. Food was also more abundant on the plains. Up to the mid-1870s, large herds of buffalo still migrated into Canadian territory, providing many plains peoples with a steady food supply and thus facilitating larger groups.

Greater organization and social control were demanded by the nature of life on the plains. The horse, especially, contributed to the development of a more organized political structure, as it led to a highly mobile society. This was in contrast to the isolated woodland bands who still moved on foot. The buffalo hunt required many horsemen, who needed to be tightly co-ordinated in the annual pursuit. These factors made it necessary to have a firmer political organization. In the spring, when all the people gathered together before the buffalo hunt, a council of men elected a chief. As a result, the plains people could be readily mobilized for both political and military purposes.

In the years after European contact, basic First Nations social structures and belief systems did not undergo as dramatic a change as did their economic base. After more than two centuries of contact with European culture, the Indian way of life still stood in stark contrast to Euro-American culture. The plains tribes adapted to the economic changes they first faced with the arrival of the horse, then the gun, then the traders. But at its core, Aboriginal culture absorbed change on its own terms and retained beliefs and practices that enabled it to thrive on the plains.

Until the disappearance of the buffalo strained the relationship, the Métis were one group that was on reasonably good terms with the plains tribes, with whom they often intermarried. Métis and Canadian free traders are known to have used the Cypress Hills regularly from the start of the nineteenth century. Indeed, the Cypress Hills is an incorrect translation of the French *montagne aux cyprès*. *Cyprès* means cypress in standard French, but for French-Canadians and Métis it was the word used first for the jack pine and then for the lodgepole pine. A number of early sites are known to have been occupied by Métis families, and it has been estimated that there were approximately fifteen major Métis settlements and campsites throughout the Cypress Hills.

A number of Métis established themselves along the Whitemud River, some of whom are thought to have been émigrés from Red River before 1869. As well, some of the Métis leaving Red River after 1870 settled in the Cypress Hills area. Among this group was Riel's adjutant general, Ambroise Lepine, who settled near Elkwater Lake on Ambroise Flats. Four major Métis camps are known to have existed by the late 1870s: one at East End (the present-day community of Eastend), one along Battle Creek near the future site of Fort Walsh, and two more at Head of the Mountain. There were also a number of smaller camps located in numerous coulees throughout the Cypress Hills.

The colonization of the Cypress Hills by Euro-Canadians has taken place in the much more recent past. In the mid- to late-nineteenth century there were only a few white traders who worked along with the Métis as fur traders and suppliers of pemmican to what was left of the declining fur trade. In the 1870s, the North-West Mounted Police arrived in the Cypress Hills to attempt to secure the Canadian half of the plains for settlement by Europeans. The police were followed by ranchers, who began to raise cattle on the rangeland in and around the Hills. It is the story of those who traditionally used the Hills and those others who later came to the area to trade and settle that is the primary focus of this book.

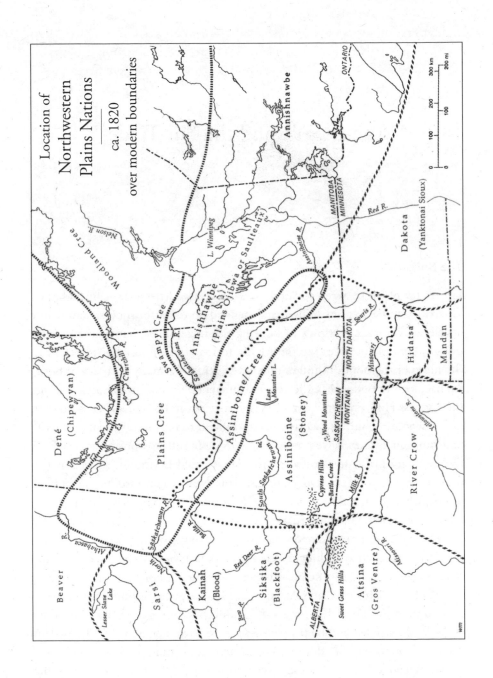

Location of
Northwestern
Plains Nations
___
ca. 1820
over modern boundaries

Beaver

Dené
(Chipewyan)

Woodland Cree

Sarsi

Kainah
(Blood)

Siksika
(Blackfoot)

Plains Cree

Swampy Cree

Annishnawbe
(Plains Ojibwa or Saulteaux)

Assiniboine/Cree

Assiniboine
(Stoney)

Annishnawbe

Dakota
(Yanktonai Sioux)

Hidatsa

Mandan

River Crow

Atsina
(Gros Ventre)

Lesser Slave Lake

Athabasca R.

North Saskatchewan R.

Bow R.

Red Deer R.

Battle R.

South Saskatchewan R.

Cypress Hills

Battle Creek

Wood Mountain

Last Mountain L.

Saskatchewan R.

Churchill R.

Nelson R.

L. Winnipeg

Red R.

Assiniboine R.

Souris R.

Missouri R.

Milk R.

Sweet Grass Hills

Missouri R.

Yellowstone R.

ALBERTA

SASKATCHEWAN
MONTANA

NORTH DAKOTA

MANITOBA
MINNESOTA

ONTARIO

0   100   200   300 km
0   100   200 mi

wm

23

CHAPTER TWO

The Buffalo and the Fur Trade

The Buffalo

Life on the plains between 500 and 1700 CE revolved around the bison herds. The tribes in the Cypress Hills area depended on them for their survival, and developed complex methods of hunting the huge herds that roamed across the southern plains. The two most basic forms of bison hunting were either the jump or the pound, though of course there were many varieties of both. Archaeological evidence indicates that ancient hunters in the area around the Cypress Hills preferred driving bison into natural or constructed pounds rather than using jumps, because it was difficult to find terrain that lent itself to a jump site. Pounds were most likely to be found in wooded areas where the necessary brush to construct drive lanes could be found, as well as the timber necessary to construct corrals. This was in contrast to the buffalo jumps, which required rim-rock over which bison could be driven. Jump sites tend to be located closer to the Rocky Mountains.

The Gull Lake pound site on the northern fringes of the Cypress Hills has turned up some remarkable evidence. Here, artifacts of three distinctive groups have been uncovered for the pre-contact period of the northern plains. Fluted points of the Plains and later Avonlea and Prairie peoples indicate their presence in the area as buffalo hunters. Algonquian-speaking Besant — a Middle Woodland (Avonlea Points) people — seem to have merged with Athapaskan invaders around 100 CE, dominating the area until approximately 700. Much of the buffalo killing at this time was done with the bow and arrow that the Athapaskans brought from eastern Canada. Makers of Prairie points, likely

Algonquian speakers, began to displace the established groups hunting with the older Avonlea points. Eventually the Prairie side-notched points emerged as the dominant buffalo-hunting technology. By 1300 CE, the Plains side-notched variant of the Mississippian culture to the south appeared and seemed to dominate until the contact period with Europeans around 1700.

The bison-hunting culture of the mid-eighteenth century encompassed four tribes that occupied the southern Canadian plains. These large tribal units would have hunted the bison with traditional bow-and-arrow methods, as well as with the gun traded down through Hudson Bay onto the plains from the seventeenth century on. The four major nations were the Gros Ventre, the Nakoda (Assiniboine), the Blackfoot, and the Plains Cree.

The Blackfoot Confederacy traditionally occupied southern Alberta, though in the eighteenth century they moved up into Saskatchewan as far as the Eagle Hills, controlling an area between the North and South Saskatchewan rivers. At the height of their military power, they occupied areas of southern Saskatchewan and north to the Battle River. The Gros Ventre occupied an area to the south and east of the Blackfoot, and likely occupied southern Saskatchewan for lengthier periods of time than the Blackfoot. The Nakoda, traditionally an extension of the Dakota people, inhabited an area east of the Gros Ventre and south of the Plains Cree, predominantly the area of northern Minnesota and southern Manitoba, but at the height of their power they extended as far north as Fort Carlton and as far west as the Cypress Hills. The Plains Cree were one of the most dominant groups on the prairies, occupying southern Manitoba and Saskatchewan and extending into southern Alberta at the height of their influence in the nineteenth century. All four of these nations would have occupied territory in and around the Cypress Hills.

Even though Europeans had crossed the Canadian plains since the late seventeenth century, the first observation of a buffalo pound was made in 1772 by Mathew Cocking, a trader for the Hudson's Bay Company (HBC). The first observation of an actual hunt in progress was made by Alexander Henry the Elder, who was travelling with the Nakoda in central Saskatchewan:

> About forty men and a great number of women . . . proceeded to a small island on the plain . . . women pitched a few tents . . . the chief led his hunters to its southern end where there was a powder enclosure. The fence was about four feet high, and formed of strong stakes of birchwood, raffled with smaller branches of the same.[1]

Henry recalled robed runners leaving at daylight to entice the herd toward the pound. Bellows imitating the bison lured curious animals toward the decoys until they were a short distance from the pound. When the animals were between the wings of the chute, the runners disappeared into movable portions of the chute walls and the buffalo gradually moved toward the pound entrance as the chute narrowed toward the corral. If bison veered from the course, people along the walls shook buffalo robes to put them back in the main stream

of the herd. Once the buffalo were inside the pound, a string was pulled, sending a curtain made of buffalo robes over the entrance to prevent escape. Henry remembered seventy-two bison killed on the hunt he observed.

Into the nineteenth century, plains people such as the Cree, Saulteaux, and Nakoda were still using the buffalo as their economic mainstay, and many tribes were increasingly selling pemmican to fur-trade company posts. As the buffalo moved less frequently onto the northern plains, the HBC became more dependent on tribes to the south of them, in the vicinity of the Cypress Hills, to supply them with buffalo meat. In return for pemmican, the Company traded guns, knives, metal, cloth, pots, beads, liquor, and tobacco.

With the increased need for pemmican, the number of hunts undertaken by the Indians increased, but not the number of buffalo killed at a given hunt,

---

LEFT: PORTRAITS OF SASKATCHEWAN INDIAN LEADERS BY EDMUND MORRIS. *These four men who frequented the Cypress Hills played prominent roles in the history of the Western Plains in the 19th and early 20th centuries.*

TOP LEFT: *Piapot (Payipwat), a Plains Cree chief, was one of the five major leaders of the Plains Cree after 1860. Originally called Kisikawasan, he was taken prisoner by the Sioux as a child, but in 1830 was recaptured by the Cree and returned to his own people. Because he had become knowledgeable in Sioux medicine, he was named Payipwat, "one who knows the secrets of the Sioux." By 1860 he had become a respected spiritual leader and chief of the Young Dogs, a Cree band with a large Nakoda component which frequented Nakoda territory* (Legislative Building Art Collection, Government of Saskatchewan, Regina).

TOP RIGHT: *Big Darkness (Opazatonka) was a Headman in 1877 and a signatory of the Nakoda adhesion to Treaty 4 signed in the Cypress Hills. Dr. Kenny Ryan, a Nakoda medicine man, thought that Big Darkness would have been a chief at one time because of the elk horn necklace he is wearing here. Big Darkness was a traditionalist and government officials disapproved of him* (Legislative Building Art Collection, Government of Saskatchewan, Regina).

BOTTOM LEFT: *Carry the Kettle became chief of the Nakoda in 1891 at the age of 47 after the death of his younger brother, Man Who Took the Coat* (with permission of the Royal Ontario Museum © ROM).

BOTTOM RIGHT: *Big Bear (Mistahah Musqua) was known for his independent spirit, refusing gifts of tobacco and tea from HBC trader William McKay who, in 1874, had been commissioned by the Canadian government to explain to the Plains nations why the NWMP were coming. Big Bear dismissed the gesture as "a bribe to facilitate a future treaty"* (Legislative Building Art Collection, Government of Saskatchewan, Regina).

which remained at about fifty to seventy animals. The most common time for a buffalo hunt was in late summer, fall, or early winter, when the animals had been fattened from their summer grazing. On some occasions, there would be a number of drives in a season if the bison were located close to favoured pound sites. In the early summer months, stationary herds of buffalo were sometimes hunted by encirclement, requiring a large number of people. This method was used to kill only a few buffalo. Bulls were not considered desirable for eating at this time, and only cows and calves were slaughtered. In late summer, the hunting of the buffalo was done on a grand scale. It required the participation of many people in a highly organized system, as the hunt was intended to kill large numbers of buffalo.

The early-season hunt was one reason individual bands came together in the spring. By then, fresh meat was required for food, sinews and bones were needed for new weapons, hides were wanted for clothing and to repair tents, and for trade. Small wintering parties would gather in larger tribal units as various bands emerged from valleys or hills in what is now eastern Saskatchewan and western Manitoba. In open areas they celebrated survival from winter and participated in the annual thirst or Sun Dance ceremony. In the ceremony, Aboriginal people asked for the sun to give them strength for the buffalo hunt and bravery in war. It also served as a rite of passage for the younger members of the band. Throughout the late spring and summer, the bands or tribes spent time on the open prairie, replenishing their food supplies, repairing their tents with buffalo skins, and gathering materials for weapons and food preparation.

The organization required for a hunt was complex, and a division of labour was required for its successful execution. Special participants included the decoy runner, the poundmaker, and, for the Blackfoot, the holy women. Considerable spiritual ritual accompanied the hunt. The poundmaker (for the Blackfoot, the holy women) was the initiator of the hunt. When no centre tree was available, the poundmaker planted the medicine pole in the corral of the pound. Ceremonies were performed at the medicine pole and at the entrance of the pound to discover the favourable moment for the chase. The poundmaker then attached charms to the pole — usually a piece of red flannel two to three metres long, as well as tobacco and a bison's horn — and placed ceremonial objects at the entrance to the pound. Early in the mornings preceding a hunt the poundmaker beat a drum and recited hymns to conjure the spirits and appease the manitous (spirits) that guided the movements of the bison. The poundmaker would often remain at the medicine pole while the hunt was in progress. The Nakoda poundmaker White Raven hung suspended from the medicine pole for the duration of the hunt.

The hunt started when the herd was located. The process of guiding the buffalo into a funnel began many kilometres away from the actual killing ground. Stone cairns joined by people waving robes were arranged in two columns to form a corridor down which the buffalo were herded. Wide at the opening, the two lines narrowed as the buffalo were chased to their final destination: into a pound or over a buffalo jump. Another group of hunters was responsible for directing the buffalo toward the opening of the funnel and ensuring that the buffalo stayed on the course to the killing area. Whole buffalo bones lying on charcoal remains, as well as butchered bone scraps, are a common pattern to the finds at the Gull Lake pound site in the Cypress Hills, suggesting the process of burning the remains of a previous hunt prior to renewed butchering activity. After a successful hunt, there followed feasting. Failure to complete a hunt once begun had serious consequences, as precious energy would have been wasted and locating a new herd meant the loss of valuable time, especially during times of want.

After a successful hunt, weeks were spent slaughtering the buffalo, then drying some of the meat. The women made the pemmican that helped carry the tribes through the winter months. Skins and furs were also prepared by the women through the late summer and fall for winter trade. In good years, some of the pemmican was traded to fur-trading companies, as were sinews, horns, and bones. Other parts of the buffalo were fashioned into tools and implements. Some of the hides were left whole. These were known as "head and trail" robes, and were more valuable than the "split robes" that were cut down the middle and then sewn together with sinew. These hides were packed together and transported by travois until the fall, when the people moved into the hilly areas.

When the buffalo were numerous, the hunts meant abundant food, but life was obviously more desperate when the herds could not be found, as was the case toward the end of the nineteenth century. When this occurred, the tribes were unable to gather enough food to survive over the winter months and they were often forced to camp by prairie lakes and live on fish they were able to catch there. This was increasingly the case for many Cree and Nakoda in the late 1870s and early 1880s. As the buffalo became scarce in Canadian territory, plains people hunted this game in smaller groups, even individually. More and more Natives who now possessed both the gun and the horse found hunting in groups less necessary.

Spring and early summer were a traditional time of war among various nations as they competed with each other for buffalo-hunting territory. In the 1870s and 1880s, the buffalo remained in large numbers in what was primarily the Blackfoot territory of southern Alberta and northern Montana. The competition for the disappearing buffalo meant that there were frequent wars between groups that sought the same herds. As the buffalo declined in number, conflicts increased as more people competed for fewer animals.

As fall arrived and the first snow of winter fell, the large tribal groupings that had moved across the plains together through the summer months would break up into smaller bands or family units and then proceed into the wintering hills. For hundreds, perhaps even thousands, of years, plains nations had wintered in forest havens such as the Cypress Hills. In the shelter of the hilly regions, among poplar and birch copses, the people were able to find fuel and could more easily pursue small game. This game would supplement the pemmican gathered in summer. Indeed, stray herds of buffalo were often found in sheltered valleys during the winter season. The people lived close to the rich resources offered by the natural world around them. They traditionally carried few material goods because these were not necessary when the surrounding land and animals provided such an easily accessible bounty.

As traders increasingly came to the area, winter was the time when the Indians and Métis came to the trading posts to exchange their buffalo robes and furs for the goods and foodstuffs offered by the traders. During the summer there was little demand for European goods. The traders arrived in the Cypress Hills in late summer or early fall with their bull-trains loaded with trade goods. If the previous year's fort was still standing, the traders occupied the same site. If not, they would choose a new spot to build on, one that might place them in a more favourable position than their competitors. As winter arrived, the traders busied themselves with the business of trade, and the plains tribes and Métis began arriving with their summer's catch.

The Aboriginal people and Métis traded for pots, kettles, traps, and other metal goods, large quantities of patterned flannel to make clothes, as well such amenities as liquor and tobacco. Many also purchased beads for their artwork and items such as mirrors simply for amusement. This trade would continue throughout the late fall and winter as the Indians looked for the best bargains they could get from the competing traders. As the winter wore on, the Aboriginal people hunted individually, pursuing buffalo and smaller game. The hides of these animals would then be taken to the traders.

Trapping for furs was now a major activity, and likewise the furs would be brought into the posts. As they depleted their own food resources, the Aboriginal people increasingly traded at the posts for food. Bacon, flour, tea, and other staples were in great demand at these times. In the most desperate years, the tribes camped close to the forts as they became more and more dependent on food from the traders. The hungrier and weaker the Indians became, the less they were able to hunt and trap.

By the late 1870s, the end of the trading season and the arrival of spring no longer meant hunting for the buffalo as it once did. This former cycle of life was over forever, and a new way of life awaited the Indians with the treaties and life on the reserves.

The HBC and the Fur Trade to 1870

The nineteenth century was a major watershed for Plains peoples. Ahead of them lay adaptation to Anglo-Canadian culture and subsistence agriculture and a life that was controlled by government regulations. Behind them lay a long tradition of adaptation to the forest and plains environments.

The Cree, who became a dominant group as a result of the fur trade, were primarily woodland people in the early seventeenth century. They occupied an area between Hudson Bay and Lake Superior, and some of the westernmost Cree occupied territories into present-day Manitoba. They were basically a hunter-gatherer band society. They used canoes, collected wild rice, and were enemies of the Dakota to the south.

Through the explorations of Anthony Henday in the mid-eighteenth century, the HBC learned that Cree to the south and west of Hudson Bay were acting as the primary middlemen in the fur trade. As they moved out of the forests south of the Bay, the Cree controlled the prairie river systems and blocked the eastward access from the plains to Hudson Bay. Not only did Henday find the Cree trading with the French, and later with the independent traders, but they were also collecting prime furs at the expense of the English.

By the 1770s, the consequences of this competition became clear. "The Indians traded their best beaver and marten inland (to the French and free traders), then came down to the company posts hoping to exchange the remnants of their catch for the Brazil tobacco and Beaver goods which the Canadians could not supply."[2]

As shrewd businessmen, the Cree were playing one buyer against the other, extracting the best prices they could for their furs. By 1773, the HBC decided to move into the interior to combat the increasing trade in furs taken by the free traders based on the St. Lawrence River. The Company moved westward in 1774, establishing a post at Cumberland House, a site between the Bay and the Saskatchewan River system and along the Athabaska river system. By the 1780s, the HBC had also established posts southward at Rainy River, Red Lake, and Lake of the Woods to make inroads into the area now dominated by its competitors. By the turn of the century, the Company was at the last barrier before the Pacific Ocean: the Rocky Mountains.

It was this move inland that weakened the stranglehold the Cree held on the fur trade that had been, until then, centred on the Bay. As the HBC moved farther inland, they were able to trade directly with the Blackfoot, Peigan, and the Blood, among others. Competition between the North West Company (NWC), headquartered in Montreal, and the HBC escalated through these years and resulted in a desperate drive to gain dominance of the trade. This had dramatic consequences for the traditional trading role enjoyed by the Cree. "As the Canadian and Hudson's Bay men moved onto the Saskatchewan, so the Western Cree and Assiniboine lost their function as middlemen in the trade, and drifted onto the plains beyond the North Saskatchewan, where they kept their links with the companies, but rather as buffalo hunters and provisioners."[3] With this displacement, the Cree again had to adjust to changing economic realities.

By 1821, the heated rivalry between the NWC and the HBC was threatening the existence of the latter. The result was a merger of the two companies, followed by an era characterized by the sound administration of the new HBC business by the energetic and efficient Sir George Simpson. Two decades later, with the demand for beaver in decline, the Company's fortunes fell. The halcyon days were gone and the Indians who had long been linked to the economic system introduced by the Europeans were not only geographically displaced, but were now economically displaced as well. A certain dependence on European goods had grown among the Cree, but while the profitability of the trade had now lessened, the demand for these goods had not. Thus, they began to look elsewhere for a livelihood.

By the time of Confederation, a national policy was in place to bring prosperity to Canada and to the West by protective tariffs, railway development, and ambitious schemes to bring settlers to the prairies. With the HBC in decline, the Aboriginal peoples and Métis were no longer able to profit from the fur trade, and the buffalo had disappeared, the last big hunt occurring in the late 1870s. The future for Aboriginal peoples depended increasingly on economic opportunities and accommodations offered by the Canadian expansion into the West. The 1870s and 1880s were a transitory period for the Plains Cree, as they began to rely on treaties, reserves, and federal government policies that promised them a new livelihood.

The role of the Cree in the fur trade, their subsequent move onto the plains after the buffalo, and the resulting diplomatic systems that emerged have only recently begun to be explored by scholars. It is perhaps a telling comment on the bias of early Western Canadian historians that comparatively little has been written about the role played by the Aboriginal peoples in the history of the fur trade.

Three distinct phases can be identified between the first direct contact with Europeans and the end of the fur-trade era around 1870. The first period began in 1670 with the alliance between the Cree and Blackfoot situated to the west. The second phase was the period when the Cree developed a stronger alliance with the Mandan to the south, who supplied them with horses. Historian John Milloy labels this phase the "Horse Wars" era, dating from 1810-50, a time when the Cree were increasingly acquiring horses and seeking alliances to the west.

During the early nineteenth century, the Cree were able to exist in their centralized tribal way of life because they maintained many of their traditional social and cultural values. Status was still gained by common activities within the nation and not by individual conquest or accumulation of wealth. They kept the tradition of distribution through gift giving and a "disdain for material possessions."[4] This was in contrast to the Blackfoot, who were growing more toward a social system based on status through the accumulation of wealth and a decentralized structure of power. The gun and horse were absorbed into Cree society without drastic changes to their social structure, although some adjustment had to take place. Tribalism remained the strongest bond for the Cree during the years up to 1850. At the end of this period, they were the most dominant nation on the plains. The once-powerful Blackfoot, enemies not only of the Kootenai, Shoshoni, and Crow, but now also the Cree, had begun to seek peace with the Cree.

The third phase is labeled the "Buffalo Wars" period of 1850-70. During these wars, the Assiniboine and Cree came together as allies against the Black-foot Confederacy. These wars were critical to the Cree and Nakoda, as fewer and fewer buffalo were coming into their territory. The years of the Buffalo Wars were characterized by dwindling buffalo herds. The Cree blamed the Métis and whites for the decline, but did not openly clash with them, since they still relied on their trade goods. The Cree partnership with the whites was no longer as useful to them as it had once been. The Cree had never been manipulated by whites, but made their own choices based on what was in their best self-interest. Buffalo was most important to them in the mid-1800s; however, they, along with their allies the Nakoda, were unable to drive the Blackfoot out from prime buffalo territory, and by the late 1870s the great herds were gone.

Indian Women in the Fur Trade

Male observers in the early contact period tended to ignore or downplay or misunderstand the role and status of women in Indian society. The observers generally fell back on images they had from their own society of women as lower-class people, and they presented Aboriginal women as slaves, drudges, and beasts of burden, indicating that they were total subordinates and under the control of men. As well, they reinforced images of women as being of questionable moral standard, emphasizing that Aboriginal marriages required no legal or religious status, that divorce was readily accepted, and that people were allowed free sexual expression from a very early age. All this was evidence of weak moral standards in the eyes of Europeans.

There have been some efforts to discuss gender relations and gender differences in Aboriginal cultures and the extent to which these were reshaped by post-colonial forces. Gender as a social construct reflects and defines the social identities of women and men. Ideas of gender provide culturally determined roles that become models for behaviour. Concepts of gender are ideological, and they explain and reinforce cultural evaluations of appropriate male and female activity and identity. The assignment of roles in society can be an indication of the gender relations in that society.

One school of thought emphasizes the egalitarian nature of pre-contact society, that Indian women were an esteemed and essential part of their societies until the imposition of Judeo-Christian beliefs. Anthropologist Eleanor Leacock, working among the Montagnais-Naskapi of Quebec, argues that in this hunter-gatherer society there was equality; that the women made essential economic contributions; that they had an important voice in the decision-making process of the band; that they had autonomy and power in domestic and reproductive concerns; that, while they had separate spheres of activity, this did not imply inequality for women; that the fact that tasks were split along gender lines did not mean that women were helpless without men, or vice versa. Men and women were mutually dependent; they controlled the terms and arrangements of their own work.[5]

The fur trade changed all this. It introduced a system of political, economic, and social organization that was incompatible with traditional Aboriginal culture. The newcomers intended to accumulate capital; the commodity they were after was fur, and they required a source of labour to produce that commodity. In order to use Aboriginal peoples as a source of labour, they had to dominate and reorganize Aboriginal society. The relationship of equality between the sexes had to end, and relations of exploitation had to replace the former relations of co-operation. This transformation took place over an extended period of time.

Those that emphasize gender inequality in Aboriginal societies before the arrival of the Europeans often suggest that European contact meant liberation to Aboriginal women; that, as their lot was improved, their prospects brightened. Many in this school of thought emphasize that women were not pawns of Europeans; that they were not used against their will; that they were "active agents" and not "passive victims." Women, it is maintained, were shrewd and pragmatic, and they adapted to the pressures of colonization. The image of women as passive victims, as pawns in the colonial situation, these scholars argue, is in need of revision. Increasingly, scholars are arguing that Aboriginal women had choices and exercised them.

In a gender study of nineteenth-century plains society among the Teton Dakota, Nakoda, Blackfoot, and Gros Ventre, Alan Klein examines the effects of the hide trade and the horse among these peoples.[6] Klein argues that these trades had far-reaching implications for the status of women. The traditional patterns of life still evident among plains peoples in the eighteenth century were remarkably altered by the nineteenth.

Klein shows eighteenth-century plains life as one that was characterized by foot travel. Collective hunting methods dominated, while individual methods were secondary. Women made vital contributions through their gathering, since the hunt was often precarious. At times, bands had to survive on the efforts of women. Klein describes these societies as egalitarian because of the nature of their hunting, which was collective. Women were required as part of the collective hunt, so their position was roughly comparable to that of men. There were also few inequities of wealth, as people produced mainly for their own use and consumption.

Changes arrived with the introduction of the horse. The horse was introduced as a privately held commodity controlled by men. Klein argues that hunting became individualized, only using large groups of hunters at certain times, as increased mobility meant that collective efforts were no longer as essential. Individual ownership of the kill was also introduced (previously the kill had been collectively owned), and the choice cuts belonged to the man who killed the animal. Women were now absent from the hunt, which had become the domain of men.

The buffalo-hide trade, introduced about 1820, introduced a new trade in European goods. This brought new technology and a new prosperity to Aboriginal peoples — and a greater demand for hides. There was also a change in labour patterns as the division of labour between the sexes became more strictly defined. To meet increased demand, there was increased specialization of labour: men became the producers of raw materials, and women became the processors of them.

The rise in the hide trade dramatically increased the amount of time women spent tanning hides. It was estimated that it took one woman approximately ten days to tan a single buffalo robe, but if she was freed from other tasks it could be accomplished in just three days. While men could provide women with raw materials with relative ease while the herds were abundant, women's work was far more time-consuming. The average man could supply at least two women with enough hides to tan. Klein sees the rise in the demand for tanners as a cause of increased polygamy. Other methods also appear to have been used to increase the labour supply, such as the capture of women from other tribes.

Ethnohistorian Richard Perry also observed that, while women's labour was at a premium, their position was in jeopardy — they laboured more and enjoyed the work less. The economy changed from one preoccupied with consumption to one that concentrated on production for exchange. There was increased prosperity, but only for men — those men who owned horses and could purchase trade goods. There was an erosion of women's position and status, while men were increasingly free to pursue wealth. Women lost the ability to control status-bearing goods. The result of all this was that, in the nineteenth century, men were favoured over women and the individual was favoured over the group. Even if women were making choices, they were still losing both political and economic status. As the material basis of plains culture altered, the egalitarian basis of plains culture was undermined by a new economic order.

CHAPTER THREE

Whoop-Up Country

The American Traders

The circumstances that brought people to the Canadian Northwest in the nineteenth century were rooted in the fur-trading activities of the first half of the century, and were propelled by the rapid rise in the price of buffalo robes in the latter half. Alcohol had long been used in the fur trade, though in the 1860s and 1870s its use became even more widespread than previously. After 1821, the HBC was largely successful in curbing the trade in Rupert's Land, although some limited use of liquor continued.[1] Alcohol was a more important part of the operations of the American Fur Company (AFC), albeit curbed somewhat by an 1832 Act of Congress prohibiting the sale of spirits in Indian territory. In violation of the law, the AFC continued to smuggle and trade alcohol, and in the hard times after 1861, whiskey smuggling helped the company stay afloat.[2]

In the late 1860s, a number of factors converged which, for a brief few years, sent the bull-trains of "Indian traders" creaking north from Fort Benton, Montana, to exploit an area that had been largely neglected by the fur trade. For a short period, until it ended abruptly on the Canadian side with the arrival of the North-West Mounted Police in 1874-75, this region received an exciting, though sometimes bitter, taste of the American "Wild West." Whoop-Up Country was characterized by the whiskey trade. South of the border it is now northern Montana, and north of the 49th parallel, southern Alberta and southwestern Saskatchewan. The expression "whoop it up" describes a run for the border by traders who sold whiskey to the Indians as they were trying to avoid being rounded up by either the army or the police. The names of Forts Whoop-Up, Slide-Out, Standoff, Robbers Roost, and Whiskey Gap illustrate the character and atmosphere of the times.

In 1862, with the discovery of gold in the mountains around Helena, what was soon to become Montana Territory boomed. When the gold rush subsided, many of the former prospectors, led by seasoned fur traders and joined by soldiers released from the Union and Confederate armies after the American Civil War, remained in the area as free traders. In 1864, Montana Territory was created and US marshals were attempting to enforce federal law. Border patrols were present, if poorly staffed. As a result, whiskey traders had to keep an eye out on the US side of the border. To evade the "long arm of the law," the Fort Benton merchants logically looked to Canada, where, although the sale of liquor to Aboriginal peoples had been made illegal by an 1867 Act of Parliament, followed by a North-West Territories Ordinance of 1870, there was absolutely no enforcement. The trading of whiskey could boost a trader's profits substantially. In 1854, a clear profit of 45 cents could be made on trading a $9.67 gun for $16.00 worth of buffalo robes.[3] Proof alcohol cost the trader $3.25 to $6.00 a gallon — diluted and spiced up, it could bring up to $50.00 in hides. In one rate of exchange, two robes were traded for one large glass of "rot-gut" whiskey.[4]

On June 15, 1870, the Helena *Daily Herald* announced that Irish-born adventurer John Jerome Healy and his business partner, Alfred B. Hamilton, had netted the impressive sum of $50,000 trading in the British possessions to the north, and concluded that this was "not very bad" for a six months' cruise among the Aboriginal peoples across the border.[5] These two businessmen from Sun River, with an estimated 200 litres of raw alcohol and backed by Hamilton's uncle, I. G. Baker, had built Fort Whoop-Up in 1869 at the junction of the St. Mary's and Oldman rivers, the first important whiskey post on the Canadian side of the border.[6] Baker was a partner in the duo's Sun River post in Montana, from which the supplies to Whoop-Up were now channeled. In the next five years or so, dozens of other traders based in Montana crossed the as-yet-unmarked international boundary and tried their luck at the risky but extremely profitable business of trading point blankets, brass wire, smoking tobacco, and diluted whiskey to the Natives across the Canadian line.[7]

It was the price paid for buffalo robes that was the traders' major motive in coming to Canada. The price of beaver declined in the 1840s and other furs became more prominent: muskrat, mink, deer, bear, raccoon, fox, skunk, and increasingly buffalo — at this time made primarily into throws for open sleighs and wagons.[8] In 1846, a buffalo robe brought a trader $3.00, a decade later $3.50, and by the early 1870s, $5.50 to $6.00, with a fine robe from Saskatchewan country bringing up to $12.00.[9] In the late 1860s, a Benton merchant could sell a number-one quality hide for $16.50 to a St. Louis wholesaler, who would then get up to $25.00 for it in the retail trade.[10] In 1871, demand for buffalo robes was further increased when a US tannery developed a new treatment to change raw buffalo skins into leather tougher than cowhide, exactly what was needed for industrial belting in the industrializing eastern United States. The hides from the northern herds were the best, being thicker than those from animals found farther south. In 1870, a total of 5,000 buffalo hides were shipped out of Canada; in 1872, T. C. Power and Co. alone sent 15,400 robes down the Missouri, many of these from Canada; and by 1876, some 75,000 were transported east from Fort Benton.[11] The robes were moved by steamboat to warehouses in St. Louis, a system that put the HBC at an extreme disadvantage, as it was unable to move the large, bulky cargoes of robes with such ease.[12]

Traders from Montana surged northward in their pursuit of the quick money the buffalo-robe trade offered. The harvest of the buffalo was pursued with such vigour that the exploitation of the herds gradually led to their depletion. Mercantile companies, centred in Fort Benton, encouraged these developments and supplied credit to traders, allowing them to venture into Canadian territory and winter on the Canadian side of the border. There they traded with the Aboriginal and Métis populations of these territories. The credit supplied to these trading partners was in the form of goods on consignment that were carried by bull-trains northward. Here the goods were exchanged with "Indian traders" for the desired furs and robes. Thus, the substructure of this trade was established along a north-south axis as traders went into Canada each season. The Aboriginal and Métis peoples occupying the territory moved in their own seasonal cycles, as the climate and terrain allowed, and in the Cypress Hills and southern Alberta they came into contact with the Benton traders.

The Hudson's Bay Company also maintained a presence in the region. Although the HBC no longer sought furs in the southern districts, where furs were now scarce, and concentrated its efforts farther north where the fur trade was more profitable, the area south of the Red Deer River remained important to the Company because of the buffalo in the region. The pemmican made from these animals made the territory indispensable to the functioning of the HBC, and they traded for it with the Indian and Métis peoples. Pemmican was the simplest way of feeding men in the territory. Its preparation remained what it had been for plains people for centuries: dried buffalo meat was placed in large troughs with berries, such as saskatoons, then melted grease was added and the whole concoction mixed with a wooden shovel. This mixture of meat, berries, and grease was then packed in rawhide bags, which were sewn shut and shipped out for use. This hearty food kept for months, even years.

Following their traditional cycles of movement, Aboriginal peoples and Métis moved to the shelter of the Cypress Hills in winter. There they sought out the crude log shacks, sometimes graced with the name "fort," constructed by the American traders to bargain for goods the traders had brought with them from Fort Benton. There were four main groups who traversed this territory. First were the plains tribes, which included the Cree, Nakoda, Gros Ventre, Blackfoot, Dakota, Crow, Sarcee, and Blood. Second, there were the Métis, who were being displaced from their once-prominent role as tripmen and freighters for the once-powerful but now declining HBC. Third, there were the traders such as Moses Solomon and Abel Farwell, who represented American commercial interests farther south. And last, there were groups of so-called "wolfers," who hunted wolves for their highly prized fur. There was usually an uneasy truce and respect, sometimes bred out of fear, that

FORT WALSH, 1878-79, *headquarters of the NWMP* (W. E. Hook, Montana Historical Society, Hook Stereograph Collection).

prevented violence from breaking out between these groups. But there were also lurking racial hatreds, especially between the wolfers and the Aboriginal peoples.

The Métis dispersed across the prairies in great numbers after the Red River Resistance of 1869-70. According to Isaac Cowie, an HBC trader in the area, many of these Métis were sympathetic to the Americans or had ties with Métis living in American territory. Thus, they gravitated toward the traders at Benton and Helena. The consequences of this were obviously detrimental to the HBC:

> The American traders were not long in taking advantage of these circumstances, and in 1872 they established whiskey trading-posts at Cypré Hills and to the west, the steam boating facilities on the Missouri giving them great advantages over us; and their acquaintance among the Blackfoot.[13]

American Métis had long provided labour, guiding, and interpreting skills for American fur-trading companies operating in the Missouri River system. Often identified as "Canadian" or "French," many actually had their origins in the Métis settlements of the Great Lakes region.[14]

By the 1870s, the Métis made up a large part of the population of the northern portion of Whoop-Up Country. Reasons for their migration west from Manitoba included discontent with the HBC fur-trade monopoly, political and social discontent in Red River, and increased demand for buffalo leather. Good prices for robes and economic goods could be found at Fort Benton because of the inland port's transportation advantage. In Canada, the diminishing buffalo herds were now concentrated in southern Alberta and the southwestern tip of Saskatchewan. All these factors led to large Métis settlements in the Cypress Hills, and at Wood Mountain, Milk River, Frenchman (Whitemud) River, and Marias River. The trade in robes and pemmican could be lucrative — one large pemmican contract for the Fort Peck Indian Agency required the meat from two thousand slaughtered buffalo — but this bounty lasted only a few short years.

By the late 1870s, the slaughter of buffalo and exploitation of game had exhausted the resources in the Cypress Hills area. The final destruction of the buffalo took but a few years: from the early 1860s to the early 1880s. The uncontrolled killing continued right to the end. By 1877, the only major herds left in Saskatchewan were concentrated south and west of the Cypress

Hills along the Milk River. Famine accompanied the disappearing buffalo for the Métis and Aboriginal peoples. In addition, a large fire in the Cypress Hills in 1879 made the presence of game, needed to support the wintering traders, scarce. By 1880, the Métis winterers of the Hills began to leave, many heading toward the Missouri River basin. Others moved to settlements along the Peace River in northern Alberta and in north and central Saskatchewan.[15] The last wild buffalo killed in the Cypress Hills was shot by Robert McCutcheon on Irvine Flats in 1882.

One group of Métis who settled in the Cypress Hills were those from the Wood Mountain area. The Métis who settled at Wood Mountain were one of two main groups who left Red River after 1869. The other, larger group of Métis settled farther south and west along the Milk River, closer to the disappearing buffalo herds. Many Métis from Wood Mountain moved west with the diminishing buffalo, and in the winter of 1875-76 the Wood Mountain community was almost totally deserted as the Métis settled in the Cypress Hills.

The practice of leaving the main settlements during winter to pursue the buffalo was one that was well known and is described as follows by a missionary:

> Our Indians and Half-breeds call "hibernation" a place they have chosen to live in during winter, and prepare themselves for hunting expeditions. To that effect, they build in the prairies temporary dwellings which they abandon at the melting of snow, and in which, meanwhile, they will find a safe cover. Usually the place is chosen only after a serious inspection. Indeed, it is necessary to find fire-wood and timber in the vicinity and, moreover, to be near the buffalo herds which supply them with meat and hides.[16]

The Cypress Hills became the temporary home for a wide variety of people as the last straggling buffalo could still be found there in winter. In previous times, only the most daring had entered into this territory without the advantage of numbers or superior weapons. The presence of both the Cree and Blackfoot was feared. But by the 1870s, Reverend Clovis Rondeau observed many different people in the Hills. Of the year 1873, Rondeau wrote:

> The place is now the perpetual rendez-vous of all Indian tribes, not only of Canada, but also of the United States. Last winter, a tribe coming

from the other side of the Missouri River had almost 1500 lodges there. The Nez Perces [sic] had 6 lodges. There were from 200 to 300 lodges of heaper [sic], Crees, Assiniboin [sic] and others. There also were the remains of a numerous tribe which, after having plundered and killed everything in certain districts of Oregon and covered a distance of 1500 miles on its flight to Canada, met the American cavalry at the frontier before reaching Wood Mountain. Those unlucky people arrived in a deplorable condition, worn out with fatigue, no shoes, no cloths [sic], no food, almost all of them wounded.

Such is the population that the hope of good hunting had attracted to Cypress Hills last winter.

There are also 200 families of French Canadian Half-breeds. That place has therefore become, during winter, a considerable centre, full of activity. The buffaloes have attracted all these people, who are a mixture of all races and religions.[17]

By 1877, the majority of the Métis who had wintered in the Cypress Hills the previous three winters had moved back to Wood Mountain. Their priest, Father Jules De Corby, identified the major Métis settlements at the Cypress Hills, Wood Mountain, Milk River, Whitemud River, and Porcupine Creek. Each settlement was estimated to have included fifty to eighty families. The constant movement of the Métis during these years was the cause of great concern for the priests and the Catholic establishment in general. Priests in the field reported that children knew only about hunting, furs, and hides. They saw the priests but once a year, and this was not enough to learn their catechism. None of them attended school:

This life of hibernation is far from being favourable to the moral and material progress of those Christians who in their attachment to the religion, often forget its precepts. In the near future, they will be compelled, although they do not want to do that, to settle down and do some farming because the buffaloes will probably disappear forever on account of the destruction of which they are the object.[18]

It was unusual to witness much violence between traders and the Aboriginal peoples and Métis, even though the over-consumption of alcohol and the disappearing buffalo did lead to isolated clashes. The relationships between groups could be amicable, if cautious, even without a police force present.

The one group disliked by both traders and Aboriginal peoples were the wolfers, whose poisoned bait, intended for wolves, killed many animals, including Indian dogs. Both whites and Métis feared the chances of escalating violence during the stressful times as the buffalo declined.

The region around the Cypress Hills was left primarily to the Aboriginal peoples and the Métis *hivernants* (winterers). By the 1860s, the latter worked as freighters on various routes through the Northwest, as tripmen on the water brigades or as employees of the Canadian or American fur-trade companies; however, their primary job was as provisioners for the fur trade as they hunted the diminishing buffalo herds. It was as pemmican provisioners that the Métis occupied the Cypress Hills. They needed to kill large numbers of buffalo, prepare their product, and then transport the goods to trading posts throughout the Northwest. Much of it went directly north to Fort Pitt, which was a major pemmican distribution point for the rest of the Canadian Northwest.

For the plains tribes, the area around the Hills had become a buffer zone, largely due to the Buffalo Wars between the Cree and Blackfoot, and the Métis moved into the gap to exploit its rich resources and to use it as a base for the buffalo hunt. The pemmican manufactured during these years was transported in Red River carts or on barges north to the Athabasca and Mackenzie departments of the HBC and northeast up the Saskatchewan River system. When the demand for buffalo leather increased, the Métis were in a strategic position to hunt the dwindling buffalo herds for the robes desired by merchants, both at Red River and at Fort Benton.

In 1870, Rupert's Land was formally transferred to the authority of the Canadian government, but this was initially little more than symbolic as there was little attempt to place a Canadian presence in the region. The HBC eventually did make some efforts to increase its fur-trading activities in southern Alberta and Saskatchewan. In the fall of 1871, clerk Isaac Cowie established a wintering post at the east end of the "Cypré Hills" at a spot called Chapel (later Chimney) Coulee. In 1873 another temporary HBC post was erected, farther north in the Sand Hills, near the Elbow of the South Saskatchewan River. The Cypress Hills were described by Cowie, at that time, as a neutral territory into which his Aboriginal guides would not venture, but also an area rich in game, particularly "red deer" (elk) and grizzly bears.

The site chosen by Cowie was ideal for winter trading, as chinook winds frequently cleared the hills of snow and made access to the fort easier. During the early 1870s, the area was in the shadow of the Blackfoot Confederacy, who did not physically occupy the Cypress Hills but frequently ventured into them. At this time Métis traders, most from Red River, were the most prominent group in the area, and were established, according to Cowie, at Wood Mountain, Pinto Horse Butte, and the Eagle Hills. Cowie remembered that some Métis were involved in the whiskey trade, but suggests that HBC traders were not.

Cowie's trade was good. In the spring of 1872, he and his Métis assistants were so laden down with furs and buffalo robes that they were forced to leave forty buffalo carcasses behind. Cowie relied heavily on the help of Métis guide Xavier Denomie, who was able to lead, by day or night, in difficult weather. The trip to Qu'Appelle in that season was expected to take two weeks, but took twice as long because of the unpredictable spring and the difficulties the horses had breaking through layers of crusted snow, produced by alternating extremes of thawing then freezing. By the end of the season, Cowie had obtained 750 grizzly bear skins and 1,500 "red deer" hides:

> Most of these were unprimed summer bearskins — mere hides which every hunter was using for cart covers instead of the ordinary buffalo bull hides, for large numbers had been slain off horseback in a run on the prairie. Many of them were of immense size approaching that of a polar bear; one skin measured by me was thirteen feet [4 m] from tip to tail. This material reservation of grizzly and elk soon ceased to them after the neutrality of the Hills had ceased owing to our invasion.[19]

The Cypress Hills were still a place of danger. Cowie indicates that many hunters and traders were shot carelessly by unskilled woodsmen who mistook their red buffalo-skin jackets for red deer. In addition, friction between various Indian groups led to conflict, and Cowie occasionally came across the remains of a camp that had been attacked. Such was the case in 1872 when he discovered a camp of careless Nakoda who had been destroyed in a raid by a band of Blackfoot. It was probably because of this and the fear of American whiskey traders that Cowie did not return to the Hills in the fall of 1872.[20]

Except for these brief forays into southern Saskatchewan, the HBC was content to keep its trade with the Cree and Nakoda centred at Qu'Appelle and Last Mountain House. Closer to Blackfoot territory, the trade was still conducted from Rocky Mountain House, but in the 1871-72 season a mere 242 robes were taken in at the fort because the Blackfoot preferred to go south to the Americans. By 1874, the post was staffed with only two men, and it was finally abandoned the following year.

Before the influx of free traders in the late 1860s, Whoop-Up Country had been visited by several parties of gold prospectors seeking gold deposits like those found in Montana. These expeditions included those of 1862 and 1864, the former sponsored by the AFC, and in 1866-67 Canadians on the way to Montana gold fields crossed the area. The best-known prospecting party was the McClelland expedition of 1868, which included John Jerome Healy as guide. At least three other future whiskey traders gained an intimate knowledge of the area with these expeditions: Joe Kipp, son of James Kipp and Earth Woman; George Houk; and Dave Ackers, the last owner of the infamous Fort Whoop-Up.[21]

The demise of the AFC in 1865 left the Missouri River basin trade open to new commercial concerns. The first of the firms that attempted to continue the trade included the small outfit of Durfee and Peck, and the Northwestern Fur Company (NWFC). However, these companies, based solely on fur trading, were unable to compete in the new environment of the 1860s and 1870s. In 1869 the NWFC abandoned the trade above Fort Buford, and in 1870 it ceased operations entirely. New, more broadly based and therefore more stable mercantile companies sprang up to fill the void.[22] Among these were Carroll and Steell; Murphy, Neel, and Co.; W. J. Wetzel; and J. D. Weatherwax; but most important were I. G. Baker and Bro. and T. C. Power and Co., the new "merchant princes" of Benton.[23]

The inland port's strategic location and Baker and Power's monopoly of the steamboat lines were the ultimate keys to success for these companies.[24] Isaac Gilbert Baker, after trading to agency Indians, was appointed chief clerk at Fort Benton in 1864. The year after the AFC collapsed, he founded a general mercantile business with his brother George, becoming "the first merchandiser in the area."[25] Their new company began supplying goods to army posts and the ever-increasing numbers of settlers and miners.[26] They soon had a rival in the trade, the company of Thomas C. Power. Power, who came West as a government surveyor, arrived in Fort Benton in 1867 with his brother. They began selling a stock of goods brought from the East to the same people as Baker.[27] These merchants drew on their business connections in the eastern US to harness the pools of capital released after the American Civil War.[28] They began to supply small itinerant traders like Moses Solomon and Abel Farwell, who dealt directly with the Aboriginal peoples.

The "Indian trade" in Whoop-Up Country changed considerably after the 1850s. The Blackfoot came to terms with the US government in 1855 with the Judith River Treaty, and any remaining aggressiveness in the tribe had been crushed by General Eugene Baker in January of 1870. In addition, Blackfoot desire for items of European manufacture had been steadily increasing since mid-century. The goods of the traders had been successfully incorporated into Blackfoot culture.[29] Factors such as these combined to break down the old Blackfoot resistance to trade.[30]

There were now two basic types of Indian traders in Montana. The first were the licensed and heavily bonded traders who traded legally with agency or treaty people, or set up at army posts. In the summer of 1868, the US government drastically limited the number of licenses issued and so I. G. Baker, on the Marias River, and the NWFC, on the Teton, became the only fur companies in the area able to legitimately conduct trade with the Indians.[31] The second group were the unlicensed traders who could not legally trade with reservation people or in "Indian territory," although what exactly that was, at any given time, was often difficult to determine. They conducted their illicit dealings wherever they could establish a trading post and attract customers.[32] These traders obtained "outfits" on credit or in partnership from merchants or licensed traders, and repaid in furs and pelts. The illegal traders usually included alcohol, a substance prohibited in the Aboriginal trade by US law since 1832, in their stock of goods.[33] The free traders soon moved into the area north of the 49th parallel where there was a total lack of policing. They diverted furs away from Red River and the HBC southward to the American companies in Fort Benton. The American traders were joined by Métis *hivernants* of such regions as the Cypress Hills, who took advantage of the higher prices offered by the American companies.

Baker and Power had founded their Fort Benton operations as the gold rush of the mid-1860s exhausted itself, and in a search for new profits these companies eagerly began to supply the illegal free traders. This trade, especially when it was extended into Canada, laid the foundations for the fortunes of the Benton merchants.[34] Power, in particular, prospered and expanded into the wholesale trade, banks, and transportation, which included the steamboats that brought smuggled alcohol upriver from Chicago or St. Louis. By 1876 he had the largest commercial enterprise in Benton, and by 1881 one of the biggest in Montana.[35] Baker, too, became wealthy. In 1874 he formed a partnership with Charles and William Conrad, becoming I. G. Baker and Co.

One eye-witness observer in the Cypress Hills was Norbert Welsh. He recalled the trading season of 1875 in some detail. Welsh established his winter camp at Four Mile Coulee. He remembered stiff competition early in the year, mainly because the American companies were able to offer a wider selection of goods than independent traders who tried to set up business. Prices paid for buffalo robes rose, and competition was intense. Welsh said: "I tell you it was very hard now to get a robe from the Indians or half-breeds."[36] By the end of March, Welsh was prepared to head back to Fort Garry with his take of the season's trade, and, in spite of the competition, he got his fair share. Welsh left the Cypress Hills with 120 good buffalo robes, 1,119 kilograms of pemmican, and 373 kilograms of dried meat. He did not make it to Fort Garry, but instead sold his goods to HBC Chief Factor Archibald MacDonald at Fort Ellice.

Welsh sold his horse for $175, the buffalo robes for $12 each, and the pemmican at 37 cents per kilogram. In total, Welsh left Fort Ellice with $600 for his pemmican and $1,400 for his robes. MacDonald had warned Welsh that prices at Fort Garry were low, and he was right; when Welsh arrived at Red River, robes were going for only $10 apiece. At Fort Garry, Welsh took his remaining dried meat in trade goods and headed back for another season. He was back out on the plains by July. He rested at Qu'Appelle then headed for Lebret. In August, Welsh took a round trip of the prairies to trade for pemmican — a total of twenty days. During this time, he accumulated 1,865 kilograms of pemmican and dried meat, which he sold to HBC trader Isaac Cowie at 37 cents a kilogram. He took half in cash and half in trade goods and headed to his wintering place in the Cypress Hills. When Welsh reached his house, he set to repairing it, mudding both his house and store-house. He was set up ready to trade by the beginning of November. He was among the last of the Canadian free traders to operate in the Cypress Hills. By 1877–78, the independent trade in the region was over.

Some of the white traders have been romanticized and described as having the dignified-sounding qualities of "independence" and "self-respect," which were highly prized and praised both by contemporaries and later commentators. While the image of the rough-and-ready "Wild West" with its gunslinger hero dominates the popular imagination for these times, much of the so-called lawlessness extended from the commercial ethic to exploit diminishing resources rather than from any inherent evil on the part of the free traders. Some of Whoop-Up Country's violence was the result of racial bigotry, especially toward Aboriginal peoples by those who hunted for wolves. The occupation of the plains by the Aboriginal peoples for hundreds of years could hardly be termed peaceful: they maintained alliances or fought for territory as the situation demanded, just as any European power did. But it was the idea of "lawlessness," of an "unpatroled" territory, that was feared by Eastern politicians and their constituents, and they believed the situation needed to be brought under control.

Frontier violence, without a doubt, had grown, and Canadian officials saw the need to avoid at all costs an international incident that might lead to American annexation of the region. There was constant tension between the wolfers and the Cree, Nakoda, and Blackfoot tribes, who were as well armed as their counterparts. It had been just one year earlier, on April 5, 1872, that four Nakoda had been massacred in the Sweet Grass Hills just south of the Cypress Hills in Montana. At least ten others were wounded when Thomas Hardwick led a group of wolfers in an unprovoked attack on a passing band of Nakoda.

It has been assumed that the independent traders whom Baker and Power backed were American Civil War veterans, recently out of uniform and prone to violence, or unemployed gold seekers eager to earn easy money

FORT WALSH, 1878: *Grizzly Bear, Mosquito, Lean Man, Man Who Took the Coat, Is Not a Young Man, One Who Chops Wood, Little Mountain, and Long Lodge* (Glenbow Archives, NA-5501-1).

by debauching the Aboriginal people with whiskey.[37] Some, but far from all, were Civil War veterans.[38] In general, those who worked at the whiskey trading posts in Canada can be divided into two classes: the traders and interpreters who had fur-trading experience in the previous decades, often with the AFC, and who actually dealt with the Indians, and the poorly paid hired men or *engagés*.

Some of the hired men had come to Montana after gold nuggets had been discovered in Grasshopper Gulch in 1861. They may have prospected, but later saw their hopes for wealth dim when the diggings played out after 1865. These men built the whiskey posts, chopped wood, and "wolfed." An examination of accessible biographical information indicates that people associated with this trade came from a wide variety of backgrounds: not only veterans but newcomers excited by the prospect of making money quickly along with experienced traders. Some of the key figures who were veterans of the Civil War were the wolfer Thomas Hardwick, and Charles and William Conrad. All three had served in the Confederate Army.[39] Two others are sometimes reported as having fought in the war, but J. J. Healy came west with the US Dragoons in 1858, and D. W. Davis enlisted in the US Army in 1867.[40] The whiskey trade was pushed forward both by restless veterans and by experienced traders.[41] A large number of traders had worked for the AFC — including I. G. Baker, Alexander Culbertson, Joe Kipp, Alexis Labombarde, Jerry Potts — or for other trading companies, like William J. S. Gladstone, who had worked for the HBC, and Abel Farwell, formerly with Durfee and Peck.[42]

American traders built at least forty-five trading locations, which included forts, posts, log shacks, sod huts, and dug-outs in southern Alberta and Saskatchewan.[43] Some traders did not construct even rudimentary shelters, but traded, mainly whiskey, directly out of wagons. In the Cypress Hills of Saskatchewan, Cowie's HBC post, established in 1871, seems to have been the first in the area, and he reported being later joined by several free traders. Cowie left the site in the spring of 1871 and indicated he did not reoccupy it because of the American traders who had established themselves there during the summer.

On May 19, 1872, one Edward McKay, a Métis, and his wife, Caroline Cook, established a trading post and farm on Battle Creek, just south of the later site of Fort Walsh.[44] Aided by two married sons and several hired men and their families, the McKays grew potatoes and barley, put up hay, and kept horses and cattle. They also hunted for buffalo and traded for robes with the Peigan, Nez Percé, and Crow in the Sweet Grass Hills, and with the local Cree, Nakoda, and Métis. When the North-West Mounted Police arrived, the McKays remained as small traders and contractors, supplying the newly established Fort Walsh with buffalo meat, and later with beef, butter, milk, and cheese, and Edward carried the mail from Fort Benton. Two of their daughters married Mounties: Jemima married John Henry Grisham Bray, and Emma married Peter O'Hare. Edward McKay died in 1884, and his body was eventually buried in Medicine Hat.

Father Jean-Marie Lestanc reported five or six trading posts in the Hills during the 1872-73 trading season. Only a handful of these are specifically known: the establishments of Abel Farwell and Moses Solomon, the post of a man named "Genoa" near East End, possibly the posts of Paul Rivers and William Rowe, and one Addison MacPherson.[45] It has been said that, in the spring of 1873, there were thirteen traders within five kilometres of Little Soldier's camp in the Cypress Hills.[46] In November 1873, following the Cypress Hills Massacre, Lestanc indicated that no American forts remained. Four or five posts were re-established in the area in 1874, but the trade ended with the arrival of the NWMP the next year.[47]

Competition for access to the lucrative trade in buffalo hides was not limited to the individual free traders, but sometimes also extended to violent attempts to force out rivals, as both I. G. Baker and T. C. Power ruthlessly pursued profit. One confrontation between wolfers of the "Spitzee Cavalry" (derived from the Blackfoot word *aapi'si,* which means wolf), led by John Evans and Harry "Kamoose" Taylor, and the traders of Fort Whoop-Up was ostensibly over the guns the latter were supplying to the Natives. Headquartered at Fort Spitzee, near High River, Alberta, the members of the Spitzee Cavalry resented this trade, since it made their own presence in the territory more hazardous. The Aboriginal people approved of the traders' presence in the territory, but disliked the wolfers. Evans attempted to force traders to sign a declaration that they would no longer supply guns to the Indians. J. J. Healy, representing the T. C. Power Co., refused, and it became evident that the Spitzee Cavalry was, to a significant degree, representing the interests of William Conrad and the I. G. Baker Co. The confrontation with Healy was thus a thinly disguised attempt to drive him out of the territory to reduce the competition for Conrad's traders.

For the most part, the trade in Whoop-Up Country was much less dramatic. American traders in the Cypress Hills, such as Abel Farwell, were occupied most of the time keeping books, trading, loading and unloading their wares, packing robes and furs, maintaining equipment and horses, hiring teams, dealing with freighters, and keeping up good relations with those who came to trade at the fort.

The Trading Cycle

The start of the trading season was one of the busiest times of the year for the traders. During the summer they had made arrangements at Fort Benton to prepare for the approaching season. The trader would begin by bargaining to secure a contract with one of the large wholesale merchants in Fort Benton. Here his skills as a businessman would be tested as he negotiated for his consignment of goods. Many factors had to be taken into account in selecting the inventory for the season. The competition between Power and Baker meant that trading experience and knowledge of the territory were important for a trader going into the field. The traders transported a great variety of goods north from the Missouri, not just staples but luxury items as well were demanded by their customers. There were basically three categories of goods: first, food and drink; second, hardware goods; and third, items of clothing and shoes.

The merchandising and warehouse interests of T. C. Power and I. G. Baker were formidable, and these merchants boasted they could supply their customers with any item that could be bought in New York. They sold everything from farm implements and mining supplies to silk, fine cloths, liquor, cigars, and perfumes. But what eventually became of greater importance to both companies was the money made from securing large government contracts from either Washington or Ottawa. These lucrative government contracts provided goods to armies, police forces, and Indian agencies. It was important for these companies to have agents in the field. Traders like Farwell and Solomon represented the companies' interests in frontier areas, where a presence had to be maintained. The ability to supply goods anywhere there was paramount, and both organizations were well aware of this. Competing traders representing rival suppliers were often found in the same vicinity, whether they set up in the Cypress Hills or in the Alberta foothills.

The most necessary of the traders' supplies were food and drink. Beef was sometimes sold in cans as corned beef, but the meat staples were generally salted, smoked, and dried bacon, carried out to the trading forts in sacks or in boxes. Other common foodstuffs included flour, tea, and tobacco. But there were also a wide variety of other items: soda biscuits, baking powder, bran,

cod-liver oil, dried apples, a variety of salted pork or ham, canned and pow-
dered milk, pepper, rice, salt, and syrup. Other canned goods were carried as
well: coffee, cranberries, salmon, beans, and oysters. Luxury items included
jams and jellies, Worcestershire sauce, and pickles. Numerous so-called drugs
were available, among them vanilla, strawberry and raspberry extracts, Epsom
salts, ginger root, and sulfur.

There was a large selection of tobacco available, with brand names such
as Flor de Canada, Laureate, Embema de Cuba, Traviata, Sara Bernhardt,
Calipe, Reyna delor Mares, Variety Fairs, Briars, Gold Flake, Prince of Wales,
and Napoleon. The traders also kept a wide variety of alcohol: English whiskey, Bourbon whiskey, regular whiskey, Hermitage whiskey, port wines, and
brandy. For the Aboriginal people, the traders usually created their own concoctions from raw alcohol, watered down with creek water, to which various
ingredients were added.

Many hardware items were popular as trade objects: ammunition, axes,
buckboards, camp equipment, chains, tool chests, chisels, churns, clocks,
horse and ox collars, curry combs, dishes, files, harness, harrows, hoes, fish
hooks, kettles, knives, lamps, matches, nails, ploughs, rakes, bull rings, scales,
screws, scythes, shovels, sleighs, snares, spoons, stoves, straps, tents, twine,
wagons, washboards, washtubs, wheelbarrows, cart wheels, wire wrenches,
and yokes.

A wide array of men's and women's clothing was also for sale: vests, shawls,
shoes, boots, shirts, pants, and dresses. Colourful cloths were popular, and
many rolls of patterned material were sold each year. Leather goods, other
than shoes, were also available in the form of jackets and coats. In addition,
felt blankets, thread, ribbons, handkerchiefs and thimbles, guns, mirrors,
playing cards, stationery, and kerosene rounded out the multitude of articles
that were traded.

The most profitable item of all was whiskey. It was usually watered down
and mixed with a variety of ingredients for taste. One standard recipe suggested adding red pepper, chewing tobacco, and molasses. Other, more elaborate concoctions included Perry Davis Vegetable Painkiller, Dr. J. Hostetter's
Stomach Bitters, Jamaica ginger, and red ink. The greed for quick profits
fueled this unsavoury trade. Though short in duration, great profits were
realized, extending right from the free trader in the Cypress Hills through to
eastern American companies with their head offices in elaborate high rises in
Chicago, St. Louis, and New York.

After bargaining and purchasing his goods in Fort Benton, the trader had

one other major task to make ready for the fall trip to the frontier: to arrange for transportation. Complications sometimes arose, since the traders were all in competition for the best teams. There can be little doubt that deals were struck and favours paid in local saloons during the summer months in order to ensure reliable transport. With teams and wagons ready, bull whackers hired, the merchandise loaded, and hay for feeding the teams aboard, the trader would be ready for the weeks of travel northward, where he would set up for winter trade. The men that supplied the transport were often Métis, who had a long tradition of acting as tripmen for goods being brought into the territory and then taking the furs and robes back to the trade centres. For the Hudson's Bay Company and the North West Company, this had been done primarily by canoe or York boat, but the tripmen readily adjusted as the fur trade moved beyond the water routes and fur-trade goods were moved overland by mule and ox trains.

The trip from Fort Benton was a slow one, taking from three to four weeks, depending on the weather and the size of the train. It would usually be made some time between late August and mid-September. This was still a season when there could be much torment from blackflies and mosquitoes, and the weather could be unpredictable.

Upon arrival in the Cypress Hills in the fall, a site to establish trade would have to be chosen. The trader would need to keep an eye out for the proximity of game and water, and have a familiarity with the territory's inhabitants in order to select a spot favourable for trading. The trader might make use of a fort occupied the previous season. If it was in a usable state, he would occupy it and begin repairs. But if he desired a new site, he would begin the process of gathering and preparing logs to begin construction. This activity would mean extra costs for the trader, as the tripmen would then have to be kept on to help with the building of a structure that usually consisted of three or four cabins and a palisade. There could be a building for the trader and his family, one for the help that would stay with him through the winter, and another that would be the trading store. The palisade was for protection, and to keep

LEFT: *Blackfoot men at Fort Walsh, circa 1878. The Cypress Hills marked the western limit of the territory of the Blackfoot Confederacy, which included the Siksika, the Peigan, and the Blood. The Blackfoot were in constant conflict with the Cree, especially in the 1870s and '80s when they were in competition for the dwindling buffalo herds* (Glenbow Archives, NA-790-2).

those who had come to trade from milling around inside. Indeed, much of the trade that took place throughout Whoop-Up Country was through a hole in the fort's palisade or door. Worn rock, and ruts from the wagon wheels of the long bull-trains can still be seen throughout the Cypress Hills area.

With the fort built and the goods unloaded, the trader would hire one or two tripmen to stay with him throughout the trading season to assist with the trade and the maintenance and supply of the fort. The merchandise had to be organized and stored to ensure that spoilage would be minimal. Once the premises were in order, there would be time to spend fishing and hunting for food to carry the fort's inhabitants through the long winter months. Ducks and geese would be heading south during the fall, and the opportunity to kill a moose or deer might present itself. Any game caught would be brought home and, in Farwell's case, prepared by his Crow wife. Other work during this season would include making sure the roofs were watertight and the chinking was in place to prevent the winter winds from whistling through the log walls. The traders were ready for the arrival of winter, awaiting the Cree and Métis to bring in their furs and buffalo robes. Winter evenings might be spent playing cards, reading, drinking, smoking, or in conversation with travellers.

As the business began, the traders would be occupied in exchanging goods for the furs, skins, and hides brought to the fort. Major tasks would include evaluating furs, bargaining, and bookkeeping. The season's trade would consist of the staple — the buffalo robe — as well as bear, lynx, marten, fox, beaver, wolf, coyote, skunk, badger, muskrat, antelope, deer, elk, and even gopher and rabbit. During the bargaining, the trader often relied on his wife or hired hands to speak with the Aboriginal people in their own language and dialect.

At the beginning of the season, the Indians usually traded for the more substantial hardware and clothing goods offered by the trader. But as the winter season began, they would be forced to trade for food as their own supplies became exhausted. Tea, flour, and bacon were preserved until well into this season, when the demand for them was highest. Alcohol was in greatest demand in the fall. In the 1870s, when buffalo were scarce in the Cypress Hills, the Aboriginal people became more dependent on goods available from these traders — and later from the NWMP — than they had been a decade earlier, when food was more plentiful. As the buffalo disappeared, there was also greater competition for other game in the region, such as elk and deer, compounding the food scarcity. Food shortages during these later years of the trade in Whoop-Up Country ensured that profits for the traders remained high.

Toward the end of winter, the traders began planning their return to Fort Benton with the season's gains. Bundles had to be made and the packing of leftover goods to be completed. Arrangements were made for transportation back south. These preparations were made around the end of May or the beginning of June. There would be a final flurry of trading as the Aboriginal people sought to obtain desired goods before they left on the summer hunt and the traders tried to divest themselves of any remaining stock. It was at just this time in 1873, as Farwell packed up ready to leave, that the Cypress Hills Massacre took place. Packed, loaded, and set to go, the laden bull-train would set off when the roads were dry enough to allow travel. The trip back would take three to four weeks.

Once back in Fort Benton, the trader again called on his business skills and instincts to negotiate with the mercantile companies for a good price for his robes and furs. To determine the profit, bookkeeping and an accounting of the winter's transactions would be completed. It was only then, for per-haps two months from mid-June to mid-August, that the trader would have a break to relax and enjoy the benefits of his labour. It was a grueling pace, but the trade in the Cypress Hills was short-lived. In the aftermath of the Cypress Hills Massacre, the North West Mounted Police arrived to end the trade of whiskey in a territory that the Canadian government had left unpat-rolled. With the arrival of the police, the border could no longer be so freely traversed, nor could the wolfers poison on the Canadian side of the border. It was the end of Whoop-Up Country north of the 49th parallel, an era that was centred on whiskey traders as agents of freewheeling American capitalism.

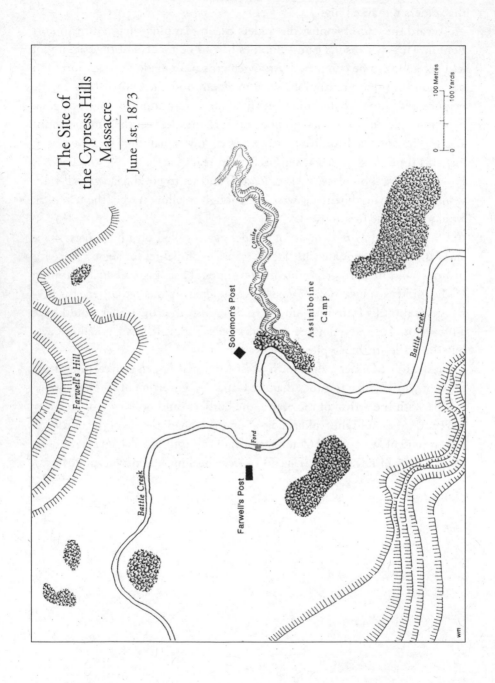

The Site of
the Cypress Hills
Massacre
June 1st, 1873

100 Metres
100 Yards

Farwell's Hill

Coulee

Solomon's Post

Assiniboine Camp

Battle Creek

Ford

Battle Creek

Farwell's Post

wm

CHAPTER FOUR

The Cypress Hills Massacre

The Personalities

The intensely competitive trade for buffalo robes and furs ultimately produced the volatile conditions responsible for the Cypress Hills Massacre of June 1, 1873. It was the theft of some horses from a party of American wolfers by Crees that set in motion the chain of events that culminated in the massacre of a group of Nakoda a few weeks later in the Cypress Hills.

For the Nakoda, led by Chief Manitupotis (Little Soldier), the winter of 1872-73 had been a hard one. Food supplies were becoming increasingly scarce for all who lived on the prairies. The Nakoda had been camped with other bands by the Battle River when their food supplies ran out in February. Little Soldier's band believed their best hope would be to move south to the Cypress Hills, and so they began a 480-kilometre trek across the frozen prairie. During this "starving time," thirty band members died.

The band finally reached the shelter of the Hills in late winter. Game was more abundant there, and the people slowly began to regain their strength. They also hoped to trade with the Americans they knew to be wintering in the Hills. The Nakoda remained there during the spring, recovering from their ordeal — an experience they shared with many other plains people at this time. At the end of May 1873, the Nakoda were camped in a beautiful valley alongside the north fork of the Milk River. There they were joined by another small band of Nakoda under Chief Inihan Kinyen. It was traditional for plains tribes to join together in the spring in larger units to hunt the buffalo, something that was becoming increasingly difficult by the 1870s. The camps of Little Soldier and Inihan Kinyen together consisted of 300 people, fifty of whom were soldier-warriors.

Close by the camp were two small log forts belonging to wintering white traders representing American companies from Fort Benton. On the west side of the creek was Abel Farwell's post, and, on the other side, a few hundred metres to the north-east, was that of Moses Solomon.

Abel Farwell (variations of this English surname include Farewell and Fairwell) was thought to have been born around 1842 in Massachusetts.[1] The heavy-set and rather tall Farwell may have been trained as a carpenter in the East, but by the 1870s he was describing himself as "a trader by occupation."[2] There is some evidence that he traded for the Hudson's Bay company on the Mackenzie River, and he first clearly appears in the historical record in 1867 as the foreman who supervised the building of Fort Peck for the firm of Commodore E. H. Durfee and Colonel C. K. Peck. The fort was constructed on the Missouri River, close to the border between the Montana and Dakota territories:

> The stockade was about 300 feet square with walls of 12 feet high of cotton-wood logs set vertically, with 3 bastions and 4 gateways in front, and two bastions on the rear. Within were various log buildings including quarters for the men, storehouses, blacksmith shop, stables, corral and even a slaughter house.[3]

SOLOMON'S POST (photo by Brian Hubner).

Fort Peck was operated as a trading post until 1871, dealing with the Nakoda and Dakota, but Farwell only traded there that season and the next. In the fall of 1869, supplied by T. C. Power, he traded at an unknown location in northern Montana or Canada. Interestingly, that same year, Isaac Cowie mentioned that, near Fort Qu'Appelle, a trader appeared who could well have been Farwell: "An American from Fort Peck, on the Missouri, got among the Indians."[4] A year later, it is thought that Farwell again came to Canada and established a post in southern Alberta on the St. Mary's River, just north of the US border.[5] In 1871, he returned to the employment of Durfee and Peck and constructed Fort Belknap in the Milk River valley. He did not trade there, the post trader being Thomas M. O'Hanlon, but worked for Durfee and Peck at Clear Creek on the Marias River.[6]

By October 1871, Farwell had a new post in southern Alberta, just above the Sweet Grass Hills. His activities there are an illustration of just how bitter the competition could get in the border trade. Farwell called in the American military because of rival John Kerler, a Canadian trader from Red River, who was with a group of Métis buffalo hunters. They were illegally trading whiskey on the US side of the line near Frenchman's Creek, a small tributary of the Marias. Two companies of US infantry duly destroyed Kerler's post in October or early November.[7]

By the fall of 1872, the thirty-one-year-old Abel was a very experienced trader. That year he obtained his supplies from T. C. Power and Co. and built a trading post in the Cypress Hills. His fort consisted of a one-room cabin with a wooden floor and two adjoining areas with upright log walls that could have been dirt-floored rooms or stockaded enclosures. The whole structure was about thirteen metres long and four metres wide, and was served by a single gate to the front. At least one cabin was attached to the rear of this structure.[8]

Some time before 1872, Farwell had married a River Crow woman originally named Goes First, known by this time as Horse Guard (although whites often called her "Mary" or "Crow Mary"). Farwell's detractors later claimed he was at this time also married to a white woman, whom he never divorced.[9] Horse Guard was born about 1855 in southern Montana, daughter of Crooked Arm or Horse Guard, a Crow man, and his wife, Strikes Plenty Woman, a Gros Ventre he had taken captive into the Crow tribe.[10] Farwell may have met Horse Guard when her people came to Fort Benton to trade. "Mary" became his partner, and assisted Farwell considerably with his trade.

Farwell had another partner that winter of 1872-73. This was George Leonard Hammond, born May 17, 1842, at St. Leonard's, New Brunswick — although in the 1880 and 1900 US censuses Hammond claimed he was born in Maine, probably to affirm his identification with the United States.[11] His great-grand-father, Archelaus Hammond, had left the US during the American Revolution and settled at Kingsclear, New Brunswick. The family prospered in their new home. Some fifty years later, George's father, A. B. Hammond, Sr., married Sarah Coombs, and then a year after her death in 1838, her younger sister, Glorianna. The Coombs sisters were also of Loyalist ancestry, and their father, Leonard Reed Coombs, had founded St. Leonard's. Sarah Hammond eventually gave birth to two girls and four boys. The lives of two of her male children — George and his younger brother Andrew Benoni, Jr. ("A. B."), both of whom left for the American West — were entwined.

George was educated in the public schools of New Brunswick and learned to speak fluent French from local Acadians. At the age of sixteen he left home, with A. B., for Bangor, Maine. The two boys had picked up the logging trade of their father, and they spent a couple of years in a logging camp in Maine before moving on to Williamsport, Pennsylvania, where they worked on the Susquehanna River. Some time in the early 1860s the two decided to "go West," and managed to get as far as St. Joseph, Missouri. In 1865, George relocated to Montana Territory. He reached Fort Benton in 1867 on the steamer

FARWELL'S FORT (photo by Brian Hubner).

Imperial, and was joined shortly by his brother.[12] George obtained a contract to supply wood to the US government from a wood yard on the Musselshell River, while A. B. remained at Fort Benton over the winter, also working as a "woodhawk," and then left for Missoula in the spring of 1868. "Woodhawks," or "wood choppers," cut and stockpiled timber along the Missouri to refuel the steamboats that plied the river. Many woodhawks also worked as wolfers in the winter months, and because of the animosity this created among local Aboriginal people, theirs could be a perilous occupation.[13] It was said that, in one year in the mid-1860s, the Dakota killed fifty-eight wood choppers on the eastern side of Montana.

In 1867, according to Old Joe Butch, a Missouri woodhawk, George helped Farwell with the construction of Fort Peck.[14] In 1868, he moved to Helena and then to Missoula, where he rejoined his younger brother. George landed a job in Hell Gate, but a year later the pair were off once more, this time taking a herd of horses to Puget Sound, Washington. In early 1870, the two brothers were back in Montana with a herd of horses, and while A. B. returned to Hell Gate, George chose to centre his activities in Fort Benton.

GEORGE HAMMOND *during his years as a Montana rancher. The theft of his horse may have precipitated the massacre* (William K. Kohrs Memorial Library, Deer Lodge, Montana).

In the 1870 census, George Hammond was listed as working as a wood chopper at a wood yard below Fort Benton. Though based in Benton, he spent much of the next three years in Canada, involved in wolfing and the whiskey trade. His short biography in *Progressive Men of the State of Montana* indicates, somewhat euphemistically, that, at this time, he was involved in "merchandising."[15] In the fall he was among those supervised by former HBC employee William Gladstone who rebuilt Fort Whoop-Up, and following its construction he remained in southern Alberta, wolfing and trading.[16] A year later, Hammond and his team of horses were members of the party led by Charles Rowe, an expedition that included the infamous whiskey trader, Fred Kanouse. The group of traders clashed with Aboriginal people on the Marias River and then built Fort Stide, sixteen kilometres downstream from Joe Kipp's Standoff Post on the Belly River.[17] When spring came, Hammond moved on to the Highwood River area and joined up with the Spitzee Cavalry gang. He was with the group that challenged J. J. Healy for control of the local fur trade. By June, George was back in Benton, where he sold his 380 buffalo robes, sixty-seven buffalo calf robes, 201 wolf pelts, and ten coyote pelts to T. C. Power for $2,796.[18]

In the 1872-73 trading season, Hammond formed an association with Abel Farwell, his old foreman from Fort Peck and a man he had been in contact with in Fort Benton. Hammond seems to have been a junior partner to Farwell. He obtained goods on credit from the senior trader and may have chopped wood and traded whiskey while Farwell worked on the accounts. Hammond may well have been the man the Nakoda called Pahazzi (Blonde Hair) — a somewhat disliked trader who dispensed the watered-down liquor and who, although he could not speak their language fluently, knew it well enough to trade.[19] Where Hammond lived that winter is unclear. He may have stayed inside Farwell's post, although the structure was not too large, or perhaps in a cabin close by with other traders and wolfers. With him lived a woman he was to marry in Fort Benton in 1874.[20]

His wife-to-be was Rosalie Wills, close to twenty years old by June 1873. It is not known where they first met, perhaps in Fort Benton or possibly in the Cypress Hills that year. She was born August 1, 1853, probably in Manitoba, although later she, like her husband, indicated an American birthplace — in her case, Minnesota.[21] In later years, a Montana old-timer recalled she was "a very pretty woman. She had some Indian blood but not very much, just enough to make her attractive. Her girls were, too."[22] Rosalie had a gener- ous and kind personality and, unusual for a woman with her background, she could read and write English, no mean accomplishment considering she never had formal schooling.

Rosalie's people were Métis who had had a long association with the HBC and the fur trade. In Canada, on her paternal side, the family was begun by her great-great-grandfather, John Favel, Jr., and his Swampy Cree wife, Titameg. Their grandson, John Richards McKay, born in 1792, traded for the HBC in Manitoba. He married Harriet Ballenden, a woman seven years his junior, daughter of John Ballenden and his Indian wife, "Jane." John Richards and Harriet had sixteen children in all, and among them were Edward McKay, the trader who established a post in the Cypress Hills in 1872, and Rosalie's mother, Mary McKay, who was born in 1820. She married John Wills, Jr., son of John Wills and Josephite Grant, on September 6, 1842. Together they had ten children, including Rosalie, and adopted one son, Alexander Wills, who was born in 1877 in the Cypress Hills.[23]

There were several additional people associated with Farwell that season. Most prominent of the workers at the post were Alexis Labombarde, Farwell's interpreter, and his wife, Nancy, who sewed and cooked. These two individuals' dramatic and interesting lives often typified the changes Métis people experienced from the beginning of the century to near its end. A French Métis, Alexis was born in 1811, son of Joseph Labombarde, his roots on his father's side stretching back into the Great Lakes region and French Canada.[24] Labombarde's mother's people were Cree. An incredible linguist, Alexis learned to speak French, English, and six Indian languages: Cree, Dakota, Nakoda, Chippewyan, Blackfoot, and Mandan. Labombarde had a lifetime of experience in the fur trade of the US and western Canada, and was perfectly at home in this environment. In 1876, he declared: "I live anywhere on the Prairie."[25] The details of much of Labombarde's early life are unknown, except that he worked as a hunter or guide at various American Fur Company (AFC) posts. He may have been the "Labonbardi" who worked as an *engagé* (hired man) at fur trade posts in Kansas around 1829, or even worked for the HBC. It is known that in 1834 and 1835 he was employed at Fort Union and at nearby Fort Clarke, in Mandan country.[26]

It was just after that time that Alexis married Nancy Kipling — or Madame Labombarde, as she came to be known. Nancy was born in 1810 in the Red River area of Manitoba, the daughter of James Kipling (also known as "Jack Ram") and his Cree wife Marguerite Okanese. By 1836, Nancy had experienced a series of traumatic events. The Kiplings were of country-born (English mixed blood) origin and worked for the HBC as labourers, guides, fishermen, and

York boat crewmen.[27] Nancy married Michel Gravelle about 1825, and had with him had two daughters: Marguerite (b. 1826), and Domitilde (b. 1828). In the summer of 1835, Gravelle worked as a clerk for the AFC at Fort Cass on the Yellowstone River, while Nancy lived with her father at Fort William, near Fort Union. Here a feud developed between Jean Baptiste Gardepied and the Kipling-Gravelle family with the Deschamps family, which resulted in the death of Francois Deschamps, Sr., in July 1835. After Michel Gravelle was killed with his brother-in-law by Blackfoot while hunting beaver on the Milk River, the Deschamps family determined that the odds had swung in their favour and decided to take revenge. In June, 1836, the sons of Francois Deschamps, Sr., killed James Kipling and shot at Nancy. The Deschamps then barricaded themselves in Fort William, but were attacked by the other men at the fort, armed with a cannon. The pitched battle that resulted ended with nine Deschamps family members dead, including the family matriarch, two or three of the attackers killed, and Fort William burned to the ground.[28] Having lost her husband and her father in less than a year, Nancy returned to Red River to marry Alexis and be baptized in the Anglican Church.[29]

ALEXIS LAMBOMBARDE HOUSEHOLD *at Fort Union. Sketches by artist Rudolph Friedrich Kurz, 1851* (National Anthropological Archives, Smithsonian Institute, No. 2856-13).

In June, 1843, while working at Fort Pierre, Alexis hunted for the famous artist and naturalist John J. Audubon while the party travelled from the Cheyenne River area to the Yellowstone River in Montana. Audubon was eager to learn the habits of prairie wildlife, such as antelope, from his hunter.[30] Alexis also worked as a hunter for Fort Union in the summer of 1851, when the Swiss artist Rudolph Friedrich Kurz visited there. Madame Labombarde and her two daughters were employed by Edwin T. Denig to make clothing on credit for those living at the fort. The finely made clothing of Madame Labombarde was eagerly purchased by travellers.[31] Kurz questioned Alexis on Aboriginal languages, and during his stay at Fort Union he compiled a 600-word dictionary of the Mandan language.[32] As with Audubon, Kurz benefited from the knowledge the Métis people like Labombarde had of the prairies. In the fall of 1851, Labombarde drove the first wagon to reach Fort Benton from Fort Union, taking Kurz and Alexander Culbertson and his family, and returning with horses.[33] Denig renewed Alexis's hunting contract in the spring of 1852, but Madame Lebombarde had refused Denig the use of her dogs to transport goods to other posts. Because of this incident, the chief trader did not renew the Lebombarde family clothing-making contract, and so they were forced to return to Red River in April, 1852.

After the mid-1850s, the personal history of the Labombardes became more closely associated with the Cypress Hills. Alexis was hired as a guide, said to be "knowing the country well," for Governor I. Stevens's Montana Exploration of 1853-55.[34] Stevens, governor of Washington Territory, conducted a military exploration to determine a feasible route for the Northern Pacific Railroad. Labombarde was probably the "half-breed Cree" interpreter who accompanied Lieut. John Mullen to Fort Benton,[35] and he was likely part of the smaller party, including artist J. M. Stanley, which was sent by Stevens to the Cypress Hills in the summer of 1853 to hold council with the Peigan. When his services were no longer needed, Lambombarde returned to the employment of the AFC and worked out of Fort Sarpy, a post on the Yellowstone River at the mouth of the Rosebud, from at least November 1855 to early 1856. In the 1860s, Alexis probably worked at various AFC posts in Montana and the Dakotas. We know that, for a period, Alexis was an interpreter for Father Alexis Andre in Minnesota. Andre was a commissioner to the Dakotas for the US government during the US-Dakota War of 1862.[36] By 1870 he and his family were living in the Cypress Hills. In the 1871-72 trading season, Alexis, probably accompanied by his wife, worked for trader Moses Solomon in the "British Possessions." The next season, they switched their employment and went to work for rival trader Abel Farwell.

Others with Farwell included James Marshall and Andrew Peterson, the latter born in Sweden and still wolfing in 1906. These two men lived in a cabin at the rear of Farwell's Post. Other, less distinct, figures associated with Farwell include a man named Kerr and one Gary Bourke. Philander Vogle, who during that winter froze his feet, had been with Farwell on the journey north, but later resided with Solomon. Precious little information is available on these men who "worked around generally," doing jobs like chopping wood, shoveling snow, skinning animals, and baling furs for their boss, Farwell, the chief trader.[37]

Two hundred metres to the east, on the opposite side of the creek, stood the post of tobacco-chewing Moses Solomon. He was said to have been a short but strong man with a thin black moustache, light blue eyes, and a good sense of humour.[38] Forty-five years old in 1873, Moses Solomon had been born the third child of a Jewish family in the village of Beerfelden, Germany, on August 15, 1828.[39] He received both a standard Jewish and a common education, and it is believed that he apprenticed as an upholsterer before he left Germany at the age of seventeen. He arrived in New York City with his brother Sol in 1848.[40] Selling a stock of goods to pay their way, the pair reached Peoria, Illinois, the home of their sister, Esther, who had previously immigrated to the US. Apparently, Peoria offered Moses and Sol few opportunities, so they soon left to join the gold rush to California. It was not to be the last time Moses was lured afield by the precious metal. Around 1855-57, he left California for a new gold rush and probably took ship from San Francisco to the mouth of the Columbia River, and then travelled to Walla Walla, Washington, to share in the bonanza of the Idaho fields. Moses's exact movements are unknown, but it appears he followed the trail of gold from Walla Walla to Boise, Idaho, and finally to Alder Gulch, Last Chance Gulch, and Confederate Gulch, all in Montana Territory.[41]

Moses failed to strike it rich, and in the fall of 1865 he decided to try a new venture. He left the gold fields and established a trading post sixteen kilometres north of Fort Benton, across the Marias River from present-day Loma, and near the spot where, the previous spring, members of the Blood nation had killed ten wood cutters.[42] Close to the same time, Moses opened a saloon in Fort Benton. For the next twenty-six years, he was to base his numerous commercial activities at his Marias trading post. It consisted of two adjoining five-by-five-metre unpainted cottonwood cabins, with the rear room serving as a living quarters and the front as the "Indian Room," in which Moses traded for buffalo robes with the Gros Ventre, who camped by the Marias. He also used the post as a base for buffalo hunting and a host of other activities and adventures.[43]

Moses Solomon's search for profitable business activities led him north up the Whoop-Up Trail and then to the Fisk Wagon Road, both of which passed within a few kilometres east and west, respectively, of his post on the Marias.[44] Moses had posts in Canada in 1870-71, 1871-72, and 1872-73. For at least one season, probably 1870-71, he was at Fort Slide-Out, a post on the river bottom on the east side of the Belly River twenty kilometres upstream from its confluence with the Oldman River. One explanation of the post's unique name relates how, when a group of traders was warned by a Native of a possible attack by the Blood, a Dutch trader exclaimed that they had better "slide-out."[45]

Possibly in 1871-72, and without a doubt in 1872-73, Moses traded for buffalo robes in the Cypress Hills. In the fall of 1872, he established a post on the east bank of the north fork of the Milk River. He obtained most of his trade goods from T. C. Power and Co., but also bought from his rival across the creek, Abel Farwell. Moses's Cypress post seems to have closely resembled his post on the Marias River. It consisted of an L-shaped two-room cabin: in the front a five-by-five-metre Indian Room, and in the rear a five-by-four-metre wooden-floored living quarters. The post also included an attached square stockade that featured bastions. A space was cut out to watch the "Indian Room," and the gate was fastened with a "log chain."[46] The porthole and chain were clearly necessary, as Moses did not enjoy as good a relationship with his customers as did Farwell.

With Moses, from Montana, came John C. Duval, a Métis from Fort Benton; George Bell, a veteran of the American Civil War; and Antonio Amei, from New Mexico. Also at the post were Philander Vogle, who had moved over from Farwell, and John McFarlane, a hunter. There were no women at this fort.[47]

The Massacre

By May, 1873, the trading season was nearly over. On a Saturday late in the month, a train of ox carts arrived at Farwell's Post to haul his take of robes, pelts, and unsold stock back to Fort Benton. The owners or teamsters of the carts and wagons were mostly Métis from wintering camps some forty kilometres east of the post. The Métis had already been told of the tensions between the American traders and the Nakoda, and they heard of them again when they arrived to start freighting. The Nakoda had accused Solomon of cheating them, and had fired shots into his post. They threatened to "clear out" the traders, and kill them all if they resisted.

Farwell was on better terms with the Nakoda than Solomon, but this spring there appeared to be a general tension, perhaps due to the many plains peoples in competition for diminishing resources. At least one Nakoda worked for Farwell, and other Natives had helped him recover horses stolen by a passing party. One of the stolen horses had belonged to George Hammond. Other events in the Hills also contributed directly to the tense atmosphere. There had been a skirmish nearby between some Blackfoot and Nakoda, and, a couple of months earlier, a group of Aboriginal people had reportedly killed a trader just to the west of the trading posts, in present-day Alberta. These incidents — and the increasing presence of whites, who were searching farther and farther afield for the diminishing animal resources of the area — produced hostility and suspicion between Natives and whites. The tension between the Nakoda and Solomon might have ended without incident had it not been for events that had taken place two weeks earlier in Montana. A group of about a dozen wolfers, returning with their season's take, were a day's journey from Fort Benton when forty of their horses were stolen. The large number of animals had not been closely guarded, as the wolfers had not expected a raid on their camp so close to Fort Benton.

Some of this gang were the curs of the plains. Their leader was Missouri-born Thomas Hardwick, alias The Green River Renegade, who had been wounded three times with the Confederate Army. Although he married a Blackfoot woman, Close Kill, Hardwick had the reputation of being an "Indian hater," and was involved in the 1875 lynching of two Aboriginal men in Fort Benton. Second-in-command was John H. Evans, also an American Civil War veteran. He had been a captain in the Montana Militia in 1867 and was one of the leaders of the Spitzee Cavalry. The year before, Hardwick and many of the men in the Spitzee Cavalry had been involved in a fight with Nakoda known as the Sweet Grass Hills Massacre. As a group, these wolfers were later referred to as "persons of the worst class in the country."[48]

After finding that their horses were missing, Hardwick and his men attempted to give chase, but, recognizing the futility of pursuit, headed for Fort Benton instead. Here, they cashed in their furs and tried to organize a posse. There was little sympathy for them among local law officials, so they set out to find the thieves themselves, armed with their own ideas of justice. They were, however, unable to follow the trail of the Cree who had taken their horses, and, after a two-week chase, they were forced to admit the trail had gone cold.

The Cree had in fact headed toward Fort Whoop-Up in southern Alberta, but the wolfer party had headed the other way, east into the Cypress Hills.

The wolfers arrived in the Hills on the last day of May. They searched for their horses, but Farwell assured them that Little Soldier's band was poor, with very few animals of their own. The gang spent the evening drinking with the recently arrived Métis freighters. Having no particular business the next day, they began drinking again early in the morning, with Solomon joining in the festivities. There is little doubt that activity was well advanced by noon, and that the Nakoda across the creek were also drinking. In this atmosphere, it was easy for the wolfers to direct their anger toward another group, even though the Nakoda had no connection with the original theft. The wolfers may simply have been looking for any excuse for a fight, and, on the frontier, where many whites believed that "the only good Indian was a dead one," little provocation was needed.

Chief Inihan Kinyen was at Farwell's post when the wolfers arrived that morning. Someone had warned him that the newcomers might make trouble, so when he returned to the encampment he suggested that the two bands take down their lodges and leave. His suggestion was ridiculed by Wincanahe, who, along with some others, was consuming the whiskey they had been given in return for Hammond's horse. A young Nakoda eyewitness, Eashappie, later recalled: "That morning whiskey flowed like water in the camps and by mid-day the tribesmen were all hopelessly drunk." Both chiefs, Little Soldier and Inihan Kinyen, were among them.[49]

The wolfers and traders exchanged tales of atrocities committed by the Nakoda, and, as they continued to drink, they became progressively more belligerent. Around noon, the situation reached a climax when Hammond's horse went missing for a second time. Cursing in both English and French, he began shouting that the Nakoda had stolen it back — suggesting that they believed they would be rewarded with more whiskey if they returned it once more. Hammond went across to Solomon's and asked the wolfers to join him in seizing some Nakoda horses in retaliation. The men needed little encouragement. They grabbed their rifles and proceeded toward the Nakoda camp along with some Métis freighters, all of them sodden with drink. Alexis Labombarde, in the meantime, had discovered that Hammond's horse had only wandered off, and shouted this to the men who were rushing toward the Nakoda camp. Unfortunately, it was too late; by this time there were few level heads willing to listen.

It is difficult to be certain what happened from that point on. Farwell later said that he tried to dissuade the angry men from becoming violent, and when this failed he waded across the river to the Nakoda camp. He claimed that there he found a Nakoda headman and concocted a deal in which he would take two Nakoda horses as security until the missing horse could be found. Farwell knew little or no Nakoda, but swore afterward that he had made himself understood and that the headman had agreed. About then, a Métis ran across to the camp to warn the Nakoda of the approaching danger. People began to run from the camp.

As some of the Nakoda spoke to Farwell, Hammond attempted to take two horses from them, but was stopped by Bighead, an armed warrior. Hammond returned to the wolfers and some of the freighters, who by this time had lined the edge of a coulee that faced the exposed Nakoda camp on two sides. From the protection of the bush surrounding the coulee, these men were virtually unseen. Fearing the worst, Farwell told the Nakoda to scatter. Then, according to his own testimony, he went to speak to the wolfers and tried to find Labombarde, who by this time had recovered Hammond's horse — but it was too late.

Somebody, possibly Hammond, fired a shot. The indiscriminate fire at the unprotected Nakoda camp began. With Winchester and Henry repeating rifles, the men in the sheltered coulee fired volley after volley into the camp. The Nakoda tried to fight back, but having few modern weapons, it was hopeless. Men, women, and children fled from the camp. Most headed for some timber fifty metres or so to the east; others hid in the bushes lining the coulee, or crossed the river. Many were shot as they fled, including Inihan Kinyen. From distant cover, the Nakoda attempted to return fire, to no avail.

The attackers then split up. One group recrossed the river to fire on the Nakoda hidden at the mouth of the coulee. They were stopped by Nakoda gunfire. The other group, according to Labombarde, "pushed into the tents or lodges," with the Benton men firing at the camp as they went. He then saw them drag four women and a man out of their lodges. The man was Little Soldier, and one of the women was the chief's mother-in-law. Two years later, she related what had happened:

> When I and my daughter were leading her husband [Little Soldier] to the Fort he saw his father dead. He threw up his arms and . . . turning to them he said: "White men, you will know what you have done today. You never knew a Woody Mountain Assiniboine Indian to harm a white man." . . . At that moment he was shot through the heart by one of the party of Americans.[50]

The women were led away to Solomon's fort. The attackers were not content merely to kill the chief. According to Farwell and Labombarde, Little Soldier's head was cut from his body and raised on a lodge pole. That such mutilation occurred was later confirmed by a Nakoda who had witnessed the scene. After raising their grisly trophy, the men set about looting and destroying the camp.

Late in the afternoon, some Nakoda were seen moving on the hills behind Farwell's. Hardwick and four others immediately set off on horseback to attack them. As they approached the river, Ed Legrace was shot dead by a warrior concealed at the mouth of the coulee. Hardwick's party then retreated to the shelter of Solomon's post. Thus, the fighting ended. But the wolfers continued their orgy: some Nakoda women were sexually assaulted throughout the night by S. A. Harper, John Evans, and Joseph Lange, a Métis freighter. Little Soldier's wife later told how she and others were repeatedly assaulted. None expected to live.

A Nakoda recalled returning to the campsite: "After dark I went into the camp and saw a woman with her back broken; she was still alive and was trying to move but could not. It was very dark. That was all I saw."[51] Later, some Nakoda returned to the site to gather their possessions. "The whole forty lodges started off, carrying everything on our backs, all our dogs having run off. We started in the night for the end of the mountain, to the halfbreeds [the Métis winterers' camp], they treated us kindly, giving us dogs, kettles and other things."[52] The Cypress Hills Massacre was over. It is still uncertain how many people died in the attack, but at least twenty are thought to have perished.

The next day, traders at both Solomon's and Farwell's hastily finished packing. The wolfers agreed to stay until this was done, and were occupied with burning the remains of the Nakoda camp. Showing the strength of her character, Horse Guard obtained the release of four of the captive women from Solomon's Post.[53] Ed Legrace was buried that morning under one of the floors within the stockade. The traders then pulled out, and the wolfers rode off to continue the search for their missing horses. As they left, someone doused Solomon's post with coal oil and set fire to it. Farwell's post, too, burnt to the ground, the work of the departing traders or later the infuriated Indians. The valley was left deserted except for the dead Nakoda, who lay where they had fallen.

The Aftermath

News of the Cypress Hills Massacre did not reach Ottawa until late August, 1873. The government soon initiated steps to have those involved extradited from the United States and tried for murder. The case languished for a time, and then was taken up by the newly created North West Mounted Police.

In the spring of 1875, the NWMP began to look for witnesses to prosecute the perpetrators of the massacre. In the spring of 1875, NWMP Inspector A.G. Irvine found the Labombardes living in a community with other Métis and hunting buffalo on the Missouri River. Alexis was hired by Irvine for $3.00 a day as a guide and watchman, with an eye to using him as a witness in the upcoming Cypress Hills Massacre extradition trial in Helena. Irvine described him as "an elderly man of fine appearance."[54] Five wolfers were arrested and brought before an extradition commission in Helena in July, 1875. Farwell was the chief witness for the prosecution, and much of the defence's case was to claim that he was a liar. Alexis also testified. The wolfers claimed it was Farwell who had led them to the Nakoda camp, that their intentions were entirely peaceful, and that they had only fired when fired upon. As it turned out, the prosecution's case was not strong enough, and the wolfers were released. In the winter of 1875, Labombarde and Farwell returned to Fort Macleod, accompanied by Irvine, Métis scout Pierre Léveillé, and NWMP officer Sam Steele. Steele related an amusing story that described the discovery of Labombarde's ancient toque in the morning stew, and the policeman called him, "one of the old hunter *coureur du bois* class.[55] Soon afterward, two traders and a wolfer were arrested in Canada and tried in Winnipeg in June, 1876. Labombarde and Farwell again travelled to Winnipeg accompanied by NWMP officers, and testified at the preliminary hearing. Once again the government case was weakened by insufficient or contradictory evidence, and the three men were acquitted. The case was finally dropped in 1882, when it became apparent that no new evidence would be brought to light. This time the Mounties did not get their men.

There can be little doubt about whom the blame for the actual fighting rests with. As the American Commissioner W. E. Cullen said at the extradition hearing at Helena, although the "preponderance of testimony is . . . to the effect that the Indians commenced the firing . . . they were doubtlessly provoked to this by the apparently hostile attitudes of the whites. . . . An armed party menacing their camp, no matter for what purpose, was by no means a slight provocation."[56]

While the killing may not have been premeditated, there can be no excuse for its wantonness. The Nakoda were victims of racial prejudice and the General Phil Sheriden frontier philosophy of "shoot first," especially when it came to Indians. The Cypress Hills Massacre demonstrated the vulnerability of life, especially Native life, on the Canadian frontier.

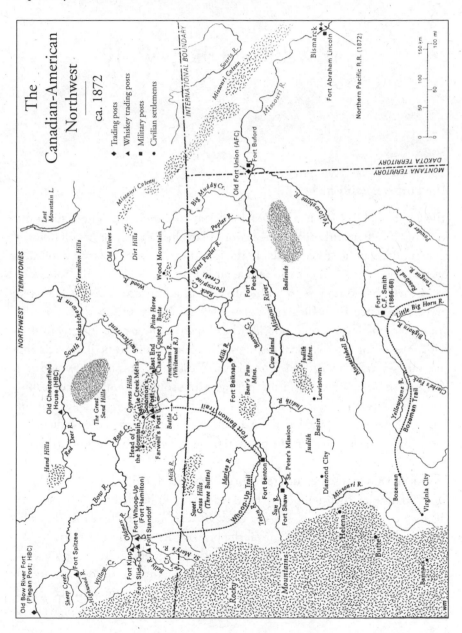

The
Canadian-American
Northwest
ca. 1872

♦ Trading posts
▲ Whiskey trading posts
■ Military posts
• Civilian settlements

CHAPTER FIVE

Fort Walsh and the NWMP

The Fort is Established

The Cypress Hills Massacre had made it clear that there was a need for some kind of Canadian authority in the region. Plans had already been laid to form a paramilitary police force similar to the Royal Irish Constabulary, established by the British government to exercise authority over Ireland. The force was to be given broad powers to both enforce and administer the law. It was to prevent violence from breaking out — for no better reason than that the young nation simply could not afford expensive military campaigns to deal with internal or international disputes. The border had to be protected and the whiskey trade controlled. The March West showed this task would not be easy. Preserving peace and preventing crime sounded eminently sensible, even necessary, in May of 1873 when the Act of Parliament establishing the force was passed; in practice, the natural environment proved as difficult to overcome as the lawbreakers the police pursued to ensure a peaceful Canadian West.

On July 8, 1874, three hundred North West Mounted Police left Fort Dufferin, Manitoba, their temporary headquarters, and headed for the territories they were to patrol. The NWMP dressed in scarlet, in the best British tradition, to distinguish themselves from the blue of the American cavalry.

The hazards of the trail soon became evident. Water was frequently scarce. After ten days of travel, the original three-kilometre line of the contingent had stretched to sixteen. There were occasions when, as the advance guard pulled out in the morning, the last of the caravan pulled into camp. Wagons breaking down as they moved across difficult terrain were the single greatest cause of delay. During hold-ups tired, hungry oxen would eat their harnesses of buckskin and collars stuffed with hay, which caused further delay. Had it not been for the hiring of Pierre Léveillé and five other Métis early into the journey to assist, the police might never have reached their destination.

The March West itself has been exaggerated to the level of mythology. The sacrifice and bravery of the men have been used to present the NWMP as the harbingers of civilization to the Northwest. As is evident from the Mounties' own reports, however, the March was a disaster, even by the standards of the day. White missionaries in the territories at the time were amused by the scores of laudatory accounts of the painfully slow and blundering move across the plains.

NWMP MÉTIS SCOUTS *Louis Cabelle and Paul Lavallie* (Montana Historical Society, 950-169).

During the winter of 1874-75 the troops of the NWMP were spread across the West from Winnipeg to the Rockies. They had marched first to southern Alberta, where indiscriminate whiskey trading had been taking place. The Mounties were still concerned about reports of whiskey trading in the Cypress Hills, and plans included the construction of a substantial fort in the Hills under the direction of Supt. James Morrow Walsh. The forts strung across the Canadian prairies during the first winter included Winnipeg, Dufferin, Fort Ellice, Swan River Barracks, Fort Qu'Appelle, Fort Edmonton, Wood Mountain, and Fort Macleod. Fort Macleod, with sixteen officers and 140 men, was by far the largest.

In the spring, Walsh had travelled to Sun River, Montana, for fresh mounts, and, under favourable circumstances, had set out for the Cypress Hills. Under the direction of scout Jerry Potts, Walsh's troop reached its objective, the Cypress Hills Massacre grounds, on June 7. A site for the fort was chosen some distance from the killing ground, in a flat area that had been cleared of brush by one of the frequent prairie fires that swept through the Hills. There was no difficulty finding timbers in the great stands of pine and spruce that grew throughout the Hills. The ground chosen was close to a creek of clear water that wound through the hilly terrain. Métis sawmen were soon busy cutting planks in the sawpits, while axmen prepared the hand-hewn logs that would serve as walls. The layout of the fort was similar to other small forts built throughout North America and closely modeled on Fort Macleod, constructed the previous fall. Stakes driven into the ground marked out the perimeter of the fort while some building exteriors served as part of the walled exterior. The buildings faced inward onto a square or parade ground.

A 3.5-metre stockade was erected by placing heavy logs 1.2 metres into the ground in trenches and packing earth and stones to secure them. The stockade was then plastered with mud and whitewashed. The walls of the stockade were reinforced by attaching square timbers onto the logs a metre from the top. The stockade enclosed an area of 95.7 metres east and west along the north side, 90.8 metres on the south side, 72.8 metres north and south on the east side and 58.5 metres along the west side. There were two bastions: one at the northwest corner and another, built later, on the southeast corner. These helped cover the approaches from the north and east. A main gateway opened to the east toward the main road to Fort Benton. Two main gates of equal strength swung into the fort on heavy iron hinges. When shut, the gates were held secure by heavy wooden crossbars, logging chains, and padlocks. Another gate opened to the creek on the west.

With an abundance of good timber available, the construction of a large number of buildings proceeded rapidly. From the southeast corner, going northeast, west along the northwest and south toward the southwest, the original buildings stood as follows: Superintendent's Residence or Walsh's Quarters, Officers' Mess, Sergeants' Mess and Quarters, Magazine, Stable No. 2, Sick-Horse Stable, Blacksmith and Carpenter's Shop, Stable No. 1, Cookhouse and Bakery, Barrack Rooms, and the Sergeant Major's Quarters. In the centre of the square stood a guardroom as well as two quartermasters' stores. There were no wooden floors built into the structures when they were first erected. Twelve-metre logs were cut for the walls of the fort buildings. At the end, they were fitted "saddle back" or "square notched" for placement on top of each other. The roofs for these log-walled buildings consisted of slender poles laid down along a central ridge pole and supported by two stringers. These poles were placed close together and covered with clay. Later improvements to the roofs included the placement of boards that were nailed to cross pieces that overlapped in board and batten style. Still later, whip-sawn lumber was nailed inside along the walls and roof, and plank floors replaced the earth underfoot. The logs were whitewashed with clay taken from the Whitemud Coulee, a few kilometres south of the fort.

A flagpole stood between the main gate and the commissioner's residence, built in 1878 for Commissioner James. F. Macleod when he made Fort Walsh the headquarters for the NWMP. A sundial was placed close to the flagpole and read daily by the trumpeter to determine the proper time for Reveille, Retreat, and Lights Out. Any Native people and Métis in the fort were expelled each day at sundown. Bunks for the men were built along the walls with white poplar poles; mattresses consisted of gunny sacks filled with hay. Windows for the building had been hauled by bull-train from Fort Benton and Helena. Latrines stood just outside the southwest bastion of the stockade. In 1879, a well was sunk between the guardroom and the west gate. The fort was completed by the fall, largely thanks to the assistance of local Métis workers.

The Life of the Mounties

The fort was run on a strict military routine. The gates were locked at Retreat and not opened again until Reveille, unless a patrol was leaving or entering (on such occasions it was opened by the sergeant of the guard) or when a civilian or Aboriginal person sought entry (on such occasions the gate was opened under survey of the officer of the day). Fort Walsh and Fort Macleod were the two major forts situated to patrol the international boundary from the Rocky Mountains to Winnipeg. This was accomplished by establishing smaller outposts from the main fort. Four subposts were to be built around Fort Walsh: Wood Mountain, East End, Pinto Horse Butte, and Milk River (Kennedy's Crossing), with summer camps at Four Mile and Ten Mile coulees. Patrols were important, as parts of the Cypress Hills were still significant gathering points for Aboriginal people and Métis hunters. In the 1870s, Métis buffalo hunters still wintered in simple dwellings at places such as Four Mile Coulee.

True to military tradition, the routine of the police resembled that of an army. The changing of the guard is a good example. Patrols entering and leaving the barracks rode at attention and gave eyes right or left when passing the flagpole hoisting the Union Jack. NWMP funerals were accompanied by the gun carriage in the military tradition, with the customary graveside volleys. This was as the creators of the Mounted Police, a true paramilitary outfit, intended. Mounted and foot drill, artillery drill, sabre and lance drill, were all carried out in military fashion. Visitors such as US general A. H. Terry were honoured with full military trappings. When Aboriginal leaders from surrounding tribes arrived for official meetings, sentries were posted, and the sentry at the gate presented arms. On unofficial visits, an orderly accompanied requests to the officer commanding.

The ordinary routine of the fort was undramatic, and this perhaps explains the high desertion rate from the force in the early years. An average day began with the orderly recording the weather: "Freezing very hard," "Weather frosty," "Thaw set in and temperature rose 25°." The morning would then be taken up with:

Reveille	6:30 a.m.
Stables	7:00 – 8:00 a.m.
Breakfast	8:15 a.m.
Office	10:00 a.m.
Parade	10:30 a.m.
Stables	11:30 a.m. – 12:30 p.m.
Dinner	1:00 p.m.

Afternoons included various drills and fatigues, among which would be carbine-revolver drill, barracks inspection, riding school, shingling stables and buildings, as well as other repair "fatigues." An ordinary afternoon would be divided into:

Guard Mounting	1:45 p.m.
Parade	2:00 p.m.
Tea	4:30 p.m.
Stables	4:45 – 5:30 p.m.
Retreat	4:45 p.m.
Picquet Mounting	5:30 p.m.
Night Guard	5:30 p.m.
First Post	9:30 p.m.
Last Post	10:00 p.m.
Lights Out	10:15 p.m.

Food was also monotonous, and the plain daily diet of the men may have contributed to their boredom:

	lbs.	oz.	grams
Beef or Bacon or Pemmican	1	8	681
Flour	1	4	568
or Bread	1	8	681
or Biscuit	1	4	568
Potatoes	1	4	568
or Beans	1	4	568
or Dried Apples		2	57
Tea		½	14
Coffee		½	14
Sugar		3	78
Salt		½	14
Pepper		1/36	1
Rice		1	26

Time in the evening might be spent in the music room, listening to concerts or singing or reading the wide variety of material available at the fort; a considerable amount of reading material was ordered at all NWMP posts. Legal statutes and texts were, of course, a necessary part of any officer's library. Any number of contemporary books and magazines might also have been found in Assistant Commissioner A. G. Irvine's bedroom, since such material was so important "to while away" time, especially in winter.

A number of books were known to have been at Fort Walsh. Among them were titles by Marryat, Ainsworth, Bulwer Lytton, Cooper, Thackery, Lever, Dickens, Samuel Lover, Sir Walter Scott, and James Grant. A large variety of magazines and newspapers were also present at Fort Walsh, including *Canadian Militia Gazette, Grip, Seasides, Cosmopolitan, Lippincott, Family Library Quarterly, Chambers Journal, Capells Magazine, All the Round, Canadian Monthly, Sunday Magazine, Canada Farmer, The Field, Scientific American, Young Men of Great Britain, Le devoir Canadien, Le courier de Montréal, The Dominion Monthly, The Saskatchewan Herald, The Mail,* and other eastern newspapers.

Games were another means of passing the long hours of winter. While many outdoor games were played in summer, such as cricket, tennis, croquet, and soccer, indoor games were more common in winter. These indoor games would have been kept in the commissioner's residence, perhaps in Irvine's sleeping quarters. Billiard tables were available at a number of NWMP posts, and other games were played, such as cards, bagatelle, backgammon, chess, draughts (checkers), and dominoes.

FORT WALSH, 1878. *For centuries, plains nations had traveled to the Cypress Hills to harvest lodgepole pine for tipi poles and for horse and dog travois. The once-thickly treed hills were quickly denuded when the North West Mounted Police arrived and used the wood to build the fort and for fuel* (Montana Historical Society, 947-451).

Distances on the prairies were immense, and duties consisted primarily in patrolling large, empty expanses. Fort Macleod was 320 kilometres to the west, and Fort Benton, where the mail run was, was 288 kilometres south. Fort Benton was also where the Mounties obtained their supplies and where the banking was done; it was also the location of the nearest telegraph.

When Commissioner James F. Macleod, successor to the first commissioner of the NWMP, George A. French, made Fort Walsh his headquarters in 1878, it had 139 men and was by far the largest fort of the five that existed at the time. With the presence of Sitting Bull in the Fort Walsh area that year, the percentage of the force's men at the fort was forty-two per cent, but by 1881 it was down to thirty-three per cent, and by December 1882 it had fallen to twenty-seven per cent. By the time the detachment was moved to Maple Creek, it was only eleven per cent.[1] Other forts in existence at the time were Fort Macleod, Fort Calgary, Fort Edmonton, and Fort Battleford.

The arrival of the NWMP may have signified the end of the whiskey trade, but not of commerce. In fact, a different trade began to flourish with the Mounties, still along the north-south axis, and, as before, with American-based companies as the prime suppliers. The Mounties made their first contact with the Americans on their march west. As the Mounties plodded onward, they ran into numerous obstacles: floods, snowstorms, stampeding horses, and men unprepared for the hardships. By the fall of 1874, they still had not made the progress anticipated. With winter approaching, the police were desperate for shelter. They sought and were given refuge at Fort Benton. Here, Commissioner G. A. French, Macleod's predecessor, forged a friendship with I. G. Baker that was to last for many years. This relationship would reap significant dividends for the American merchants. Contracts won by them, sometimes in the face of equal bids from Canadian firms, would help pull the Montana merchants out of the depression in which they had found themselves after the decline of the buffalo-robe trade.

The obvious choice for providing the police with supplies was the Hudson's Bay Company. For a variety of reasons, however, the HBC was unable to establish itself effectively as an alternate supplier. Charles John Brydges, land commissioner for the Company from 1879-89, wrote that the influence of the I. G. Baker and the T. C. Power companies was preventing the HBC from securing contracts. Although Brydges laid the blame for this on bribery on the part of the I. G. Baker Co., he quietly admitted in his correspondence that the Company, at least in the early years, did not have the capacity to supply goods to the NWMP. It was more convenient, in any case, to have supplies brought through a system that was already established. In these early years, when survival was the predominant consideration, economic nationalism was rarely mentioned, and sentiments favouring loyalty to Canadian companies fell on unsympathetic ears. Only the prime minister, Sir John A. Macdonald, lent consideration to such arguments, and was able to wield his influence in some cases.

The value of contracts awarded by the Canadian government was considerable. In 1880, contracts amounting to $100,000 were up for tender; in 1881, $400,000; in 1882, $500,000 — all substantial injections into a frontier

NORTH WEST MOUNTED POLICE, FORT WALSH. *The Mounties liked to be photographed with Aboriginal people or wearing native garb to show friends and family what the West was like* (Glenbow Archives, NA-1535-1).

company, substantial enough to warrant bribery on the part of I. G. Baker to ensure that his company secured the contracts. The HBC was eager to move into the commercial retail trade and to diversify its traditional reliance on the fur trade. In 1880, Brydges wrote to London:

> The entire change which is about to take place in the position of the Mounted Police and the Indian Department in the North-West, affords the company a very favourable opportunity of obtaining a very large share indeed of that trade. If the opportunity is not taken advantage of this year, it will pass into the control of other parties.[2]

Brydges's fears were well founded, for the competition and the presence of Baker did affect the fur trade:

> By allowing Stobart, Eden and Co., Baker and others, to get [the] hold they have of the general trade in certain districts, they are becoming powerful competitions in the fur trade, considerably reducing the profits of that trade. A good many of the officers realize this fact now.[3]

Baker exercised an influence over the Canadian-based Stobart, Eden and Co., alowing him in some cases to avoid paying tariffs on goods coming directly from the United States. Through this Canadian subsidiary, Baker had a virtual monopoly on the lucrative contracts made available from the Canadian government.

The HBC, however, received political assistance in getting established from "Sir John," as Brydges referred to the prime minister. Unlike the NWMP, who continued to award contracts to American merchants, Macdonald, at least in this case, was motivated by a feeling of nationalism. As Brydges explains:

> Our tenders Sir John told me, were about $50 in aggregate higher than Baker's, but he gave it to us because he did not want the Americans in. He wishes we would next year tender for every place and then, we would shut out Baker altogether because of his paying bribes to Smith and Kavanaugh.[4]

The influence of I. G. Baker lasted until 1891, when the I. G. Baker Co. sold its business and merchandise in the North-West Territories and real estate in Alberta to the HBC. Before the disappearance of Baker from the prairies, and while American merchants were still enjoying a virtual monopoly in the North-West, Fort Walsh retained a significant position in the operations of the police. More importantly, in terms of material culture, the Mounties bought most of their goods south of the border. Indeed, when the NWMP moved to Maple Creek, the T. C. Power store relocated with them. The relationship was, in effect, a *quid pro quo* whereby T. C. Power supplied the police with goods and, in return, the police provided these merchants with protection.

Before the NWMP arrived, there was no significant or permanent retail trade in the Cypress Hills area; there was simply no stable population or demand to risk establishing this sort of commercial enterprise. Then, with the presence of the federal government in the form of the NWMP, survey parties, and the Indian Department, a new economic order was established, characterized by a heavy dependence by local merchants on the business provided by government agencies. The government agencies attracted Aboriginal people and Métis, who became a prime market for the merchandise of the retail merchants. Even though the economic flow of goods remained through the north-south axis between Fort Benton and Fort Walsh, the primary cultural influence was eastern Canadian. Despite this, distribution from the east was still arduous, and the cost of obtaining supplies exclusively through Canada was prohibitive in both time and money.

A town rapidly grew up around the police fort, partly because of the protection the fort offered but primarily because of the market the policemen presented. As a result of the police presence, many First Nations people and Métis were also drawn into the area. Some came for protection and rations, but most came to collect their annuity payments. As a local merchant named Marsh often observed in his letters to Fort Benton, "The money spent by the Indians [their annual treaty] will amount to about $12,000."[5] Goods sold to the Aboriginal people and Métis included blankets, clothing, shoes, food, and tobacco, as well as items considered luxuries, such as mirrors.

The character of the town that sprang up around Fort Walsh in the late nineteenth century resembled a ramshackle shanty-town. Buildings were strewn in the Battle Creek valley in no apparent order. They represented an unconscious structural response in an environment where survival was still the primary consideration. As Wallace Stegner has written, this primal motivation results in a deceptively practical appearance: "People on a frontier revert quickly except when they are preserving some nicety, to folk skills, and some of these are so primitive that they seem to have scarcely any national character at all."[6] The function of most of the buildings reveals that the town was essentially a warehouse centre. While the local laundry, the restaurant, and the hotels provided essential services, the pool halls and the local tailor could satisfy hedonistic or fashion desires.

The police investigated many crimes at Fort Walsh, but the most sensational concerned the death of Constable Marmaduke Graburn, who was shot in a coulee just to the west of the fort on November 17, 1879. Graburn was found shot through the back of the head at a campsite to which he had returned to retrieve an ax. From the beginning, the police were convinced that Graburn was shot by a member of a band of Bloods who had camped in the vicinity some days previously. The evidence used to connect the suspect, Star Child, to the crime, was, even in the beginning, slim at best. Regardless, Star Child was doggedly pursued until he was apprehended two years later. The police could hardly be accused of impartiality in the conduct of their investigation. In the police reports, Star Child was described as "a particularly insistent mendicant — a pinched-faced, evil eyed Indian of small stature, who, while given to profuse self-praise and boastfulness; was not above eking out a livelihood by sheer beggary."[7] But even such demonizing was not enough to convict Star Child. Two years after the killing, a jury of six Albertan ranchers who heard the evidence against him at Fort Macleod were unable to convict him.

That there might have been other, perhaps even white, suspects, even fellow Mounties, which should have been investigated, apparently never occurred to the police. If there was any doubt about the perpetrators of frontier crimes, it seems clear that the police always looked for their man among the "regulars" they seemed perpetually to be "rounding up." Thus, the process of hegemony, of imposing Anglo-Canadian standards on "the lesser breeds" who were seen as being without the law, in part explains the confidence of the police in pursuing their duties as vigorously as they did, even in instances where caution might have been better advised. A sense of mission was rarely lacking in paramilitary forces like the NWMP. After all, the force was modeled after British examples that had been effectively used throughout the empire.

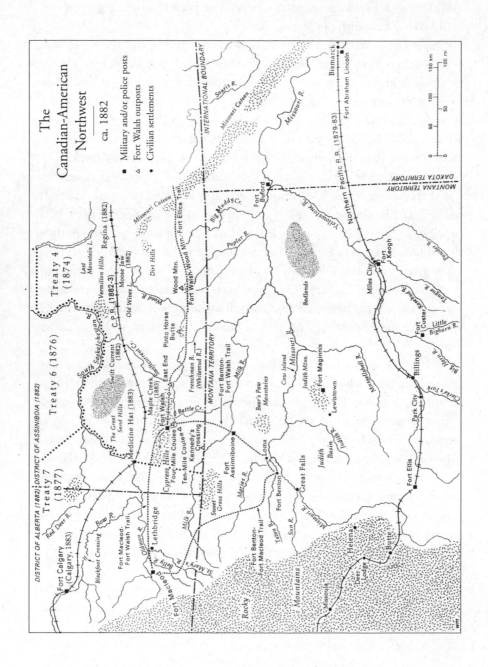

The
Canadian-American
Northwest
ca. 1882

■ Military and/or police posts
△ Fort Walsh outposts
• Civilian settlements

INTERNATIONAL BOUNDARY

Souris R.

Missouri Coteau

Bismarck
Fort Abraham Lincoln

150 km
100 mi
100
50
50
0
0

Northern Pacific R.R. (1879-83)
MONTANA TERRITORY
DAKOTA TERRITORY

Missouri Coteau
Fort Ellice Trail
Big Muddy Cr.
Fort Buford
Missouri R.

Treaty 4
(1874)
Regina (1882)
Last Mountain L.
Vermilion Hills
C.P.R. (1882-3)
Moose Jaw (1882)
Dirt Hills
Old Wives L.
Wood R.
Wood Mtn.
Fort Walsh-Wood Mtn.
Fort Walsh (1882-3)
Poplar R.

Yellowstone R.
Fort Keogh
Miles City

Treaty 6 (1876)
South Saskatchewan
Swift Current (1882)
The Great Sand Hills
Maple Creek (1883)
Pinto Horse Butte
East End
Fort Walsh
Frenchman R. (Whitemud R.)
Milk R.
Missouri R.
Badlands

Fort Custer
Little Bighorn R.
Big Horn R.
Rosebud R.
Tongue R.
Powder R.

DISTRICT OF ALBERTA (1882); DISTRICT OF ASSINIBOIA (1882)
Treaty 7
(1877)
Medicine Hat
Cypress Hills
Four-Mile Coulee
Ten-Mile Coulee
Kennedy's Crossing
Battle Cr.
Fort Benton-Fort Walsh Trail
Loma
Fort Assiniboine
Bear's Paw Mountains
Cow Island
Judith Mtns.
Fort Maginnis
Lewistown
Judith Basin
Musselshell R.
Billings
Park City
Clark's Fork
Fort Ellis

Red Deer R.
Fort Calgary (Calgary, 1883)
Bow R.
Blackfoot Crossing
Fort Macleod-Fort Walsh Trail
Lethbridge
Oldman R.
Belly R.
St. Mary's R.
Milk R.
Sweet Grass Hills
Marias R.
Fort Benton-Fort Macleod Trail
Teton R.
Fort Benton
Sun R.
Great Falls
Missouri R.
Judith R.
Judith

Rocky Mountains
Missoula
Deer Lodge
Helena
Butte

wm

CHAPTER SIX

Treaties and Reservations

The Prairies in Transition

In the early 1870s, as the buffalo herds diminished, the Cree, Nakoda, and other Aboriginal groups had no choice but to turn to the Canadian government in Ottawa for assistance — a government that was offering to settle them on reserves in return for title to their lands. Some turned to agriculture to try to alleviate starvation, but crop failure and government regulation were to make these attempts difficult. More frequently, Aboriginal people sold furs to independent American traders who had established their posts across the southern Canadian prairies. Some of these traders, and the commercial concerns that had backed them, remained and continued their trade in these territories even after the arrival of the NWMP, but the Native people were finding fewer and fewer hides and pelts to trade with them. Their options for survival were running out as Sir John A. Macdonald's National Policy, with its aim of a West settled by Euro-Canadians, closed in on them.

What is clearly evident from the life of the Cree at this time is that they remained a functioning and vital people. As historians Arthur Ray and John Milloy point out, they were never directly the victims of Europeans or other First Nations, but consciously and rationally adjusted to new circumstances.[1] However, through the years they were increasingly presented with new problems. Milloy emphasizes that, by 1870, the Cree were as powerful as they had ever been, and were in a strong position to meet any challenges put to them. They had an enviable military and diplomatic record as they faced the Canadian state that was moving westward. In the past, they had often faced new economic and military situations and had come through each crisis: from their life as woodland people to the first contact with Europeans, from their adaptation to the gun and horse to their role as middlemen in the fur trade, and finally as plains buffalo hunters. All these changes had not dramatically affected their internal social dynamic.

In the eyes of Euro-Canadians, the ironic tragedy for the Aboriginal people in the 1880s was not their new dependence on the whites but that they had not internally changed to become a materialistic, accumulating people. Such a change would have facilitated their adaptation to the capitalistic society in which they now had to live. They had outlived the buffalo on the plains and the spiritual strength derived from this close contact with nature was now more distant as they settled on reserves. What had served them so well for hundreds of years would now be a hindrance:

> What was led into the bondage of reserves was not the ruin of a political and social system, but rather a healthy organism which had taken root and grown strong on the plains. The fate of the Plains Cree nation followed that of the buffalo — not to death, but into a white man's pound, the reserve.[2]

In the early 1870s, the prairie nations were still following annual cycles based on the changing seasons. In the spring, plains people still emerged from the protected shelter of the woodlands and river valleys onto the plains to gather in large numbers for the annual Sun Dance, where the men asked for power from the sun and invited visions that were induced by fasting, and the young men passed from adolescence into the adult life of their band or tribe. Contacts with neighbouring groups were renewed, and military and trade strategies and policies were discussed.

After spring break-up, the people caught fish by extending weirs across streams and rivers, and in summer they lived in relative abundance off the harvest from the buffalo. Roots, berries, seeds, fruits, wild honey, wild rice, and maple syrup were plentiful, and could be collected during the late summer. The prairie turnip, or white apple, was also harvested. As autumn approached, the larger tribal unit began to break up into smaller groups and move to the protection of the parklands, away from the Blackfoot and in search of a haven from the severe winter weather. Some of the older men would go in search of large game such as moose and elk, and food was prepared to last through the winter months. Pemmican, which was high in protein and could last for years, was made and stored; often it was all that carried the Cree through the harsh winter months. Large stocks of pemmican, tallow, dried meat, and buffalo robes were set aside to trade to the Hudson's Bay Company in the spring.

Winter was accompanied by hardship. Individual members of each band or family would stalk game in the snow. In the shelter of the tents, the myths and stories of the people were rekindled, along with accounts of recent exploits, perhaps to become future legends. Crafts were also a common activity in winter, as were sports and games that included popular forms of gambling. Furs to be traded in spring were collected and prepared. After enduring the long winter nights, the Cree looked to the sky for signs of spring and rebirth as each year was lived out in response to the rhythms of nature. To them, life unfolded in cycles, and there was little sense of linear progression as each year passed.

The Christian world view brought to the plains by the European missionaries stood in stark contrast to that of the plains tribes. European Christians did not live in proximity to nature and did not seek communion with it as the Aboriginal people did. Rather, they adopted an adversarial attitude, and viewed nature with suspicion and fear. It was something to be conquered and overcome, as were their own emotional and physical desires. The Christian world view was human-centred and only incidentally concerned with seasonal cycles. The Christian God was one to be feared. According to some religious dogma, humans to appease this God would need to toil on earth and prove their worth to avoid damnation and burning for eternity in hell, a concept alien to Aboriginal religion. In Indian beliefs, an individual might be denied the fruits of a pursuit because a spirit power had not been properly appeased, but the consequence was not the eternal damnation of the Christian God.

Through their fur-trade contacts, First Nations were familiar with Christian concepts, but the European traders had not made any attempts to convert them. As missionaries began arriving, however, it was soon apparent they were intent on converting to Christianity what they saw as a heathen, savage people. These Christian missionaries, unlike Aboriginal religious men or shamans, had what has been described as a compulsive need to convert Indians to Christianity. The missionaries felt threatened by an unknown they could not control.[3]

The biblical injunctions that informed and directed the missionaries compelled them to reject Aboriginal culture and society. At the cornerstone stood the dictum from Genesis 1:2: "Be fruitful and multiply, and replenish the earth and subdue it: and have dominion over the fish of the sea; and over the fowl of the air, and over everything that moveth upon the earth." This was the directive for the Christian "sodbuster" — to "break" the soil and tame the land. By the mid-nineteenth century, Victorian Canadians had a boundless faith in their society and culture. They were proud of their railways, steamships, and factories; they were confident that during their lifetimes, man was reaching the pinnacle of his mission to subdue the earth.

The band and tribal life of most plains peoples stood in stark contrast to the more aggressive dynamic that motivated Victorians of young industrial Canada. They did not have the same concept of structured society as Victorian Canadians. Though they had often adjusted to changing circumstances, plains tribes still followed the seasonal cycles and pulse of nature and not the Newtonian clock of absolute time ticking by the second. These contrasting concepts of time made it easy for the Europeans to criticize what appeared to them as laziness, since their unit for measuring the time by which tasks were to be accomplished — the second — was much smaller than any unit familiar to Aboriginal people.

There were other characteristics of tribal society that made Victorian Canadians critical of the Aboriginal way of life. Their apparently casual attitude toward private property was quite alien to Europeans, who felt the accumulation of wealth by the individual was an important way to evaluate each person's value. The movement of people across the plains without an easily perceptible purpose was seen as evidence of a shiftless people, ill-equipped by religion and unprepared by culture to recognize the value of property ownership. Private property was seen by Victorians as a prerequisite in establishing a work ethic and the desire to strive for improvement. Hunting was not a respected pursuit to the Victorian frame of mind, unless as a sport or pastime. A lifestyle based on a feast or famine cycle was thought to be improvident, and further evidence that Aboriginal people, whose economy was based on hunting, were incapable of planning for the future. To live so close to nature and to be virtually at its mercy was an indication of a primitive society; not to accumulate a surplus proved a lack of mastery over nature. By the 1880s, as plains peoples became increasingly destitute and dependent on whites, many Canadians believed they had been proved right. To them, the inability of Aboriginal people to make the land fruitful by settling and their preference of wandering in pursuit of game was evidence of a people that did not live correctly. Indeed, their own way of life seemed to flourish next to that of the Aboriginal people.

It was the European concept of private property that was eventually to destroy Aboriginal claims to the use of the western prairie, and it was the implementation of this idea that ultimately would erode their way of life. The concept of title for land ownership was alien to the Indian peoples, yet in a short time what seemed impossible was soon realized.

Attitudes toward land use changed on the prairies during the 1870s and 1880s. The transition went from land enjoyed in common (that is, to be used by all) to open access (where land is claimed but can still be used by others) to the entrenchment of land held legally as private property. Prior to the systematic settlement of the prairies, Aboriginal society functioned on and perhaps survived through communal co-operation. They did not believe that anyone had sole rights to the resources: "Game was the common property of all, and everyone had a chance to share in this gift of nature."[4] When passing through territory held by Aboriginal people, individuals were free to take or use any resources they needed, whether that be game, water, or fuel. The plains tribes were "a people who had no notion of exclusive and permanent property rights in land or the other gifts of the Great Spirit."[5] Those with a wealth of resources in band or tribal society would share with those less fortunate; it was considered a matter of pride and an indication of status to be able to give to those who were in need. These people were in fact living amid wealth and, by the nature of their culture, did not need to be conspicuous consumers. Their environment was rich with resources: wood, water, forage, game, fish, berries, honey, wild rice, clothing, housing, weapons, implements, toys, and thread. To have access to all this, however, great freedom of movement was required. Farming, which meant a sedentary life, was only incidental to plains life, and agricultural products were usually obtained by trade. Plains peoples thus moved with the seasons, following the migrations and cycles of the wildlife.

Most obviously disruptive to this lifestyle was the disappearance of the buffalo herds, which led the Aboriginal people to a greater dependence on other food sources and agriculture. Their movements were restricted not only by this development, but also by the increasing settlement of the plains. At first, through the 1870s, those Aboriginal people who had not yet signed a treaty protested against white settlers and interlopers who simply occupied territory and gave nothing back in return. It is not clear if they understood the settlers were actually claiming the land. "Emphasis was on the use of lands — indeed, it seems probable that the Indian thought of the problem as that of the right to use their lands . . . the outright sale of those lands was a concept entirely unfamiliar to them."[6] Gradually, more of their resources, such as fish, wood for fuel, and game, were not only being depleted but exploited.

European discourses concerning Indians were unsympathetic, especially when describing the culture and society of plains people. Europeans had equated living in harmony with nature as "savage" and exploiting nature as "civilized." But Aboriginal land use and movement with the seasons were in fact evidence of a dynamic, adaptable way of life, quite in contrast to the images of a largely moribund and static people that Europeans presented:

> Native economies in America were not poorer, more precarious, or more miserable than their contemporary European counterparts. Indeed, recent studies of hunting and gathering societies suggest that natives of the western interior may have lived a life of relative comfort and plenty.[7]

The Downstream People and Treaty 4

The Aboriginal people who commonly used the Cypress Hills area at the time the North West Mounted Police arrived in the West were mostly the Downstream people who eventually took reserves in the Qu'Appelle Valley. The Downstream people of the Touchwood Hills, File Hills, and Qu'Appelle Valley were distinguished from the Cree who lived north of the South Saskatchewan River, or the Upstream people. These people were Saulteaux, Nakoda, and Plains Cree. A western group of these Downstream people — the Calling River People — were regularly found in the Cypress Hills in the 1870s. They often wintered in the Hills near Old Wives Lake and Swiftcurrent Creek.

One of the main chiefs of the Downstream people, recognized as the head chief of the Touchwood People, was Kawakatoose — Poor Man, or Lean Man. He was noted as a brave warrior, and it was said that he had gone to battle armed only with a lance made of a shoot of a saskatoon bush and topped with an iron head. His band participated in the famous battle of the Belly River in 1871, in which twenty of his people died. Other significant chiefs of the more easterly bands were Kaneonuskatew, He Who Walks on Four Claws, or Gordon, as well as Kisecawchuck, or Day Star. Day Star's band were known particularly for repelling an attack of the Blackfoot at Red Ochre Hill near Swift Current. Three hundred Blackfoot died, while only fifteen Cree fell. Other well-known chiefs included Kakeesheway, or Loud Voice, who was acknowledged as the head chief by the HBC. He was highly regarded as a medicine man and military strategist.

Of the more western bands were the people of Kahkewistahaw, or He Who Flies Around. This band hunted in an area that included the Cypress Hills. Kahkewistahaw was a distinguished scout, hunter, warrior, and linguist. He was not highly regarded by the HBC, however, and therefore was not likely heavily dependent on the fur trade. Another band that hunted in the Cypress Hills area was that of Chief Cowesses, or Little Child. Among his members was the distinguished Saulteaux spokesman, Louis O'Soup. Other chiefs who occupied this more westerly territory included Pasquah, whose band was predominantly Saulteaux.

Chief Piapot's Young Dogs or Little Dogs, a large band of Cree-Nakoda people, also lived off land west and south of the Qu'Appelle country. Piapot was thought to have important contacts with the more southerly Nakoda. Piapot's band in particular hunted in the Cypress Hills area, and also to the south as far as the Missouri River and north up to the South Saskatchewan River. As the buffalo disappeared, this group ventured farthest west in search of the diminishing herds. Piapot's band wintered in the Wood Mountain area and frequently in the eastern Cypress Hills as well. He was thought of as an honourable chief by the HBC, but was also viewed as ambitious and troublesome. Again, he was likely more independent of the fur trade than some of the more easterly Downstream people. Others among the chiefs who moved throughout this territory were White Calf, Peepeekis or Little Black Hawk, and Little Black Bear. The latter was a noted warrior and Cree leader at the battle of Red Ochre Hill.

These were the groups that were to sign Treaty 4. By the end of the 1870s, the food crisis had led missionaries in the area to refer to the situation among these people as appalling. The disappearing and receding buffalo herds had already led many of these Indians to supplement hunting with agriculture even before the signing of Treaty 4. Many people of these nations were already familiar with agriculture, and were knowledgeable about their environment: the extent of the growing season, rainfall and frost patterns, soil varieties, the availability of water, pasturage, and the local vegetation. They were well acquainted with the care of domesticated animals through their experience with their horses. By treaty time, however, starvation had reached such proportions that it was clear to these people that they would require government assistance in order to make the transition to an economy based on agriculture.

In the pre-treaty years, there were many suggestions from Ottawa by civil servants as to how to solve the problem of starvation and settlement of the Aboriginal people. Most of the suggestions were made by bureaucrats who had never been to the West, and most of whom knew nothing about Native people. Their suggestions ranged from turning Aboriginal people into a pastoral people who would tend horses and cattle, to having them work on railroad crews, or as guides or constables for the police and the military. Lessons had been learned from earlier treaties, and John Christian Schultz, for one, argued that more money had to be spent by the government to ensure a proper transition to the agricultural way of life advocated for Aboriginal people. Schultz criticized the "paltry" annuity payment given in Treaties 1 and 2, and suggested more land be given — sixty-four hectares instead of sixteen, as stipulated in previous treaties. Schultz also recommended a sum of money be set aside from the land sales so that the people could be given an education.

In spite of the many grand suggestions, "the government disregarded the advice not only of Schultz but also of those who advocated the unique needs and characteristics of the people of the North-West to be taken into consideration in devising policy."[8] The government, instead of reconsidering existing policy, took the path of least resistance and simply adopted for the West the same approach they had taken to the treaties in the East. Large tracts of land were to be transferred to the Crown in advance of colonization. In return for relinquishment of title, the Aboriginal people were to receive annuities, reserves, and guarantees that they could continue to hunt on portions of the land they had given up to the Crown.

Amid fears that settlers would begin arriving before land issues were settled, and amid apprehension about the presence of the telegraph, railing, and survey crews, First Nations began to pressure the government about its intentions for dealing with Aboriginal people. In 1874 Chief Poor Man sent his brother, Kanocees, to speak with Alexander Morris, lieutenant-governor of the North-West Territories, about the necessity of settling many issues that concerned the Aboriginal people. Thus, the plains peoples took an active role in negotiating with the government. They were determined to have their voice heard: "By interfering with the survey, and preventing the construction of the telegraph, the Plains Indians made it clear that they would not allow settlement until their rights were fully recognized."[9] The other major concern of the Cree, Nakoda, and Saulteaux leadership was that they be able to develop a new base of economic security for the future. This is clear from the speeches made by chiefs during the negotiations. Sweet Grass, an eloquent spokesman, stated the Indian position to Morris:

We heard our lands were sold and we did not like it; we don't want to sell our lands; it is our property, and no one has a right to sell them. Our country is getting ruined of fur-bearing animals, hither to our sole support, and now we are poor and want help — we want you to pity us. We want cattle, tools, agricultural implements, and assistance in everything when we come to settle — our country is no longer able to support us.[10]

Even though the government claimed its bargaining position was fixed and that it did not have the ability to alter terms of specific treaties, Aboriginal negotiators were able to pressure Morris to agree to a number of items of great concern to the Downstream people. Initially, the government had offered only reserves and annuities, but the Aboriginal negotiators demanded and secured the promise of implements and farm animals.

The negotiations that marked the Qu'Appelle treaty (Treaty 4) took place in September, 1874. The government representatives consisted of Lt. Gov. Alexander Morris; David Laird, minister of the interior; and W. J. Christie, retired chief factor of the HBC. The Qu'Appelle people chose Loud Voice as their main spokesman. Among the three main groups — the Cree, the Nakota, and the Saulteaux — it was the latter who bargained most vigorously. The Gambler, a Saulteaux chief, demanded that the issue of the HBC and their land be dealt with before any other items were settled:

They claimed that the three million pounds paid by Canada to the company should rightfully be theirs. They did not want the company trading in their territory, except at the posts, and they asked that the debts owed by the Indians to the company be cleared as some compensation for the company's profits from the transfer of their land.[11]

It was not until six days of negotiations passed that agreement was reached, and this without the influential bands of Piapot and Okanese present. Agriculture was thus to be the basis of new reserve economies:

To any band thereof who are now actually cultivating the soil, or who shall hereafter settle on these reserves and commence to break up the land . . . two hoes, one spade, one scythe, and one axe for every family so actually cultivating; and enough seed, wheat, barley, oats, and potatoes to plant such lands as they have broken up; also one plough and two harrows for every ten families so cultivating as alone said; and also to each Chief, for the use of his band as aforesaid, one yoke of oxen, one bull, four cows, a chest of ordinary carpenter's tools, five hand-saws, five augers, one cross-cut saw, the necessary files, and one grindstone.[12]

By the time Treaty 6 was signed two years later, even more assistance for reserve agriculture was contained in the agreement. Treaty 6 signatories bargained for more spades and hoes, more ploughs and harrows per family, more livestock, a handmill, and an incentive of $1,000 paid to each band that was cultivating the land three years after signing the treaty. The additional assistance demanded by Treaty 6 signatories was a clear indication of their determination to see agriculture become a successful basis for a new economy, but it was also as a result of witnessing the difficulties Treaty 4 people were having: "They were aware of the limited progress made by the Treaty Four [sic] Indians, who did not have such provisions."[13]

On September 4, 1877, at Fort Walsh, the Nakoda bands of Long Lodge and Man Who Took the Coat agreed to sign an adhesion to Treaty 4. The story of the Nakoda and Treaty 4 are more fully dealt with in chapter seven.

Sitting Bull and the Dakota in Canada

The numbered treaties of 1871-77 had dealt with removing the threat of "Indian uprisings," at least in the minds of government officials. Métis discontent continued to fester, however, since their land claims remained unsettled. In the meantime, an unexpected and potentially disastrous problem for Canadian authority in the Northwest was the appearance of the Dakota (Teton or Lakota Sioux) in Canadian territory after they had destroyed an American military force commanded by Lt. Col. George Armstrong Custer at the Little Big Horn. The American method of dealing with Indian populations differed dramatically from the Canadian approach. What Canadians hoped to achieve subtly, the Americans chose to achieve by force. In 1876 the Americans spent $20 million fighting "Indian Wars" — wars that literally cleared the land for white occupation. Canada could not afford such a solution; force was not only an expensive option, it was an impossible one. The numbered treaties, negotiation, and dialogue were the Canadian responses to the Aboriginal populations. The Mounted Police were the Canadian sign of authority, not the blue-coated cavalry that the Americans sent out to hunt down the Indians.

In conflicts at the edge of expanding empires, a frontier altercation, however small, is an excuse for large-scale reprisals. This usually happens with the first settlers or proselytizing missionaries who are mistreated or worse by local Aboriginal populations. In the American example that brought the Dakota to Canada, it was neither God nor Glory that produced a fearful military response, but gold.

The disputed territory that eventually led to the Battle of the Little Big Horn was the Black Hills, now in South Dakota. The Dakota had always been a powerful tribe made up of many subgroups. The plains people of the Dakota had always moved about the American plains and even up into Canadian territory as the strength or weakness of groups on their fringes allowed. The Dakota also had historical connections with Canada, dating back to the War of 1812, when they sided with the British to fight American forces in the West in a war that was crucial in preserving British, and eventually Canadian, territories from being annexed by the United States. The Dakota thus felt they had a right to Canada's protection in their own time of need.

Sitting Bull, or Tatanka Iyotank, the spiritual leader of the Dakota, earned his name as the result of a fight while he was still a youth. In tribute, his father gave him his name, Sitting Bull, and took for himself the name Jumping Bull. In 1857, at the age of twenty-six, he had become one of the war chiefs of the Hunkpapa and one of the most influential leaders among the various Dakota tribes.[14] In spite of the legends about his military prowess, however, Sitting Bull was more renowned as a medicine man or political leader among his people than as a warrior.

With the Dakota in 1876, during their conflict with the American government, were a group of Nez Percé, so called for their pierced noses. The Nez Percé had already come into conflict with white settlers in the mid-nineteenth century, when settlers began to invade their territories throughout Oregon, Washington, and Idaho. A treaty had been signed with the Nez Percé; however, it took four years to ratify the treaty, which was to protect territories in these regions for use of the Indians. The discovery of gold in 1861 brought hundreds of prospectors onto Nez Percé lands. The government ignored the 1855 agreement and replaced it in 1861 with an agreement that gave mining privileges to the gold diggers. A new treaty, drafted by the government in 1863, took away seven-eighths of the land originally granted to the Nez Percé peoples. The Nez Percé chiefs, Joseph, Looking Glass, and White Bird, refused to sign the new treaty. The legacy of lies and betrayals that the Nez Percé had endured would also be the fate of the Dakota farther to the east.

The Indian Treaty of 1851 with the Dakota had protected their territories in the Big Horn Mountains from intrusion. The Dakota repeatedly asked that the Bozeman Trail run to the west, so as to leave their hunting grounds unmolested. When the requests for negotiation went unheeded, a series of massacres and battles ensued throughout the territory. Among the most famous of these battles was one that took place in 1866, in which the Dakota were led by Chiefs Red Cloud and Man-Afraid-of-His-Horses. Whites already suspected that gold might be found in the hills occupied by the Cheyenne and Dakota, and the greed already exhibited by gold-seekers would undoubtedly mean excursions into these areas.

The Dakota had sworn among themselves that no one would reveal the presence of the gold they knew to be in the Black Hills. Eventually, after much bloodshed and acrimony, the United States government and the Dakota sat down to negotiate the Laramie Treaty of 1868. In this treaty, the US government agreed to set aside lands and hunting grounds onto which no white could trespass without permission. Territories north of the Platte rivers and east of the Big Horn Mountains were designated as "Indian Territory." The forts in Dakota and Cheyenne territory were to be abandoned. Despite this treaty, the military presence in the territories continued, as did hostilities against the Indians. George Custer became famous for being an Indian fighter when he led an attack on the camp of Chief Black Kettle in the Washita Valley in 1868. Many military leaders throughout the West adopted a confrontational attitude toward the Aboriginal peoples of newly created territories and declared open season on any Indian people found outside designated lands. It became clear that they intended no peaceful resolution to disputes over mining territory set aside for Aboriginal people. The negotiated truce in the end mattered little, and whites continued to trespass onto Aboriginal lands. The military were unable to stop these incursions, and often sided with the white settlers and gold miners. The Dakota were being antagonized and provoked to act against the many violations of the treaty. As a result of the constant breaches of the agreement, the United States government sent Custer into the Black Hills to choose sites on which to establish forts — ostensibly to keep the peace. When Custer returned from his mission, he reported the presence of large gold deposits in the Hills. The result was predictable, and gold-crazed prospectors streamed into the Black Hills. As one US military official wrote, "There never was a wilder grab for gold than the succeeding dash into the Black Hills in the face of solemn treaties."[15]

With the discovery of gold, the US government attempted to keep the

Dakota out of the Hills, but they refused. In response to the violation of the treaty and the resulting chaos, Sitting Bull called for armed resistance. Along with Crazy Horse of the Oglala and Gall and Rain-in-the-Face of the Hunkpapa, he began to gather his people along the Powder River.

As discouraged and starving Dakota began to join the ranks of Sitting Bull and Crazy Horse, the US government issued an ultimatum, declaring that any Aboriginal people who did not return to their allocated reservations by January 31, 1876, would be regarded as enemies of the state, and force would be used to return them there. The order had been issued on December 6, 1875, and compliance was impossible.

The army was ordered to proceed against those in violation of the ultimatum. When spring arrived after the extremely difficult winter of 1875-76, the Dakota faced an army eager to contain and then defeat them. The command of the American forces was given to Brig. Gen. Alfred H. Terry with support from Col. John Gibbon, Gen. George Crook, as well as the 7th Cavalry of Lt. Col. George Armstrong Custer. There was to be no quarter given. The campaign against the Dakota and the Cheyenne was to be complete and decisive: the people would return to the reservations or the military would force them there. The US armies moved against the Native people from the north, east, and south. Early in the confrontation, Crook attacked a large camp of Dakota and Cheyenne at Rosebud Creek, but was unable to defeat them. The presence of large and determined American military forces led some chiefs, such as Red Cloud, to return to their reservations, but not the determined Sitting Bull and his followers.

The strategy of Terry was to locate and approach Sitting Bull's men and to attack only when every avenue for escape had been blocked. Converging armies were sent into the Big Horn Mountains. The commands of Gibbon and Custer were to meet in the Big Horn Valley on June 26. They were still unaware of the setback Crook had suffered at the hands of Crazy Horse on June 17.

The land between the Rosebud and Powder rivers was searched to locate the large concentration of people under Sitting Bull's leadership. On June 24, Custer, with the help of a Crow scout, found the Dakota moving across the Wolf Mountain divide. Custer's scouts warned him that the large camp they located was too big to be engaged. Ignoring this advice, Custer gave orders to advance, intending to attack the Dakota before they could escape. He divided his twelve troops, amounting to 600 men, into three columns in preparation for the attack. He did not consider waiting for Terry's or Gibbon's forces, even though Sitting Bull's fighters numbered 2,500 - 3,000.

The middle column — Maj. Marcus A. Reno with three troops — was to move down a creek valley toward the Little Big Horn and attack the village from the south. Capt. Frederick W. Benteen's three troops were to move to the left or south for a scout up the valley and then report back to the main body. Capt. Thomas M. McDougall, with one troop, brought up the rear and escorted the pack train. Custer and five troops moved parallel to Reno on the right to strike at the lower end of the village.

The planned co-ordinated attack of the columns failed, and Custer, who had advanced far ahead of the others, was surrounded and killed with 215 of his men. The Crow scout Curly was the last survivor to see Custer alive.[16] The victors then attacked Reno and Benteen, but when the day ended, the leaders of the Dakota and Cheyenne realized there would be little point in prolonging the fighting. The consequences of an Indian force defeating a whole American army would be horrendous, and the Dakota leadership knew as much. The Dakota/Cheyenne alliance dispersed, with people moving off in different directions to avoid pursuers. One group, led by Crazy Horse, moved southeast, hunted by Crook. The American military soon amassed an army of four thousand men to continue the campaign against the Dakota.

Sitting Bull had moved north toward Canada for safety. With some 1,000 people he struck fear into the commanders of the northern forts, including Peck, Belknap, and Benton. Throughout the summer and into the fall, the Dakota evaded the US armies and hunted buffalo along the Milk River. Superintendent Walsh, who was on sick leave in the early summer, returned to Fort Walsh in the fall of 1876, and, together with his scout, Louis Léveillé, tried to ascertain the whereabouts of the Dakota with Sitting Bull. So far, no refugees had been found in Canadian territory, but Walsh continued to send out patrols to locate the Dakota.

In November, Sub-Inspector Edmond Frechette encountered the Dakota near Wood Mountain, heading for Jean-Louis Légaré's trading post. Légaré was a French Canadian who had married a Métis wife and established himself as a trader in the Wood Mountain area. He became aware of the Dakota when a small group entered his post and declared that they wished to trade. Légaré and his five Métis employees did their best to supply them with the goods they wanted. About half of Sitting Bull's Dakota were there, and the remaining trailed not far behind, although the chief himself remained in Montana. When Walsh arrived in Wood Mountain in December, there were an estimated 500 men, 1,000 women, and 1,400 children camped there. By the spring, there may have been close to 4,000 people at Wood Mountain. In proximity to the refugee camp was the settlement of White Eagle's Sisseton Dakota, who had fled to Canada following the 1862 rising of the Sioux known as the Minnesota Massacres.

White Eagle was of great assistance to Walsh and the NWMP. He was able to explain to the Dakota just arrived how the police operated, and that they could expect fairness if they complied with Canadian law. The Dakota, through their great chief Black Moon, in return told Walsh that they were tired of being hunted, that they wanted nothing more than to rest peacefully in Canadian territory, and that they had no intention of launching an attack on the American forts in the northern states. The Dakota then begged Walsh for some ammunition in order to hunt, as their long trek north had left them in a state of starvation. Walsh cautioned them against using the ammunition for any other purpose, and made it clear that it could not be sent across the

NWMP Superintendent James Morrow Walsh, *circa* 1882. *Walsh is best known for his handling of Sitting Bull and the Dakota who arrived in Canada following the Battle of the Little Big Horn and settled near Wood Mountain. Some say Walsh was removed from his position at Fort Walsh because his relationship with Sitting Bull was "too good"* (Glenbow Archives, NA-1771-1).

border to aid those still actively resisting the authorities. The Dakota assured Walsh that such was not their intention, and Walsh allowed Légaré, the local trader, to distribute the ammunition — to the great relief and gratitude of the hungry Dakota.

The arrival of the Dakota on Canadian soil produced a series of problems that the Mounties had to be aware of and be ready to handle. The Dakota were traditional enemies of the Plains Cree and Saulteaux peoples, as well as of the Blackfoot. This could lead to strained relations and conflict, especially if they came into competition for the same food supplies. Luckily, in the winter of 1876 there were plenty of buffalo in the Wood Mountain area; shortages were not likely to arise in the short term, but a longer stay might change these circumstances. Also, there was the potential for problems resulting from border incidents that might bring American armies into conflict not only with the Dakota but with other Canadian Aboriginal peoples as well.

Walsh had come out to meet the first group of several thousand Dakota with but twelve men. Thus, astute negotiations and trust were what the police had most to rely on. The Mounties had to rely on the weight of their moral authority, since they were not likely to be able to settle very much through a show of force. American military authorities greatly feared further attacks from the Dakota, so the NWMP had not only to pacify and control the Dakota in their territory, but they also had to reassure the American generals (some of them anxious for reprisals) not to worry about the refugees on Canadian soil. A further issue that concerned the Mounties was whether Sitting Bull would be able to unite otherwise disparate tribal peoples into an alliance to fight the Americans and recover the buffalo hunting territory that they at one time dominated.

There were other possible situations that the Mounties had to be aware of. One of these was the potential for an alliance between Louis Riel, now living in Montana, with the disaffected people gathered around Sitting Bull. All these issues meant that the NWMP had to act carefully and judiciously both in gathering information and in interpreting the intelligence gathered. The situation throughout the Northwest became tense as buffalo migrations onto the Canadian prairies became less and less frequent. Many peoples, such as the Peigan, Blood, Sarcee, Blackfoot, Saulteaux, Nakoda, Cree, Gros Ventre, Crow, and Métis relied on this staple for survival.

Despite the presence of the Mounted Police, the Canadian West was still seen as a place where outlaws might act with impunity or escape justice from law enforcement forces south of the border, a situation which was to increase into the 1880s as the American frontier closed.

In order to handle the dangerous situation regarding Aboriginal people, Walsh increased the police presence at subposts east of the main fort in the Cypress Hills. This increased the ability of the police to keep up a proper surveillance of the Dakota refugees and helped in maintaining the communications necessary for a successful negotiated settlement of the crisis. One of these outposts was at the eastern end of the Cypress Hills, appropriately named East End, approximately seventy-two kilometers from the main fort, and the other was at Wood Mountain, 208 kilometers away. To assist with gathering information and proper communication, Joseph Morin, a Métis interpreter, was hired by the Mounties and stationed at Wood Mountain.

Skirmishes between the Dakota and the American armies in pursuit of them continued throughout the fall. Several confrontations between the Dakota and US forces included the people with Sitting Bull. Also at large were Crazy Horse and his followers, who never ventured into Canada but whose whereabouts were of great concern until their surrender on May 6, 1877, at

JEAN-LOUIS LÉGARÉ *was a French Canadian who had married a Métis woman and established himself as a trader in the Wood Mountain area. He first became aware of Sitting Bull's Dakota when a group of them entered his post and told him they wanted to trade, but his trading post was soon the centre of activity for the Dakota in Canada* (Saskatchewan Archives Board, R-A47).

Red Cloud Agency. Gradually, as starvation continued and pressure by the US military continued, the ranks of the Dakota resisting relocation were thinned.

In the spring of 1877, three thousand Dakota people gave themselves up at the Red Cloud, Spotted Tail, and Cheyenne River agencies and returned to their reservations. Three hundred Cheyenne also surrendered at the Tongue River Cantonment. Calm descended around the Wood Mountain area in the winter of 1876-77. The Dakota brought buffalo robes and other furs and skins to Légaré's trading post. He supplied them with tea, tobacco, sugar, and flour, as well as beads and decorative items. Légaré initially prospered from the trade with the Dakota, but they had increasingly fewer items to trade with and they began to ask for provisions as gifts. By 1878, Légaré was involved in efforts to get the Dakota to leave Canada, even sponsoring a feast at his own expense.

For Walsh, winter conditions made travel difficult: it took nine days to travel from Wood Mountain to Fort Walsh, a trip that took half that time in summer or fall.

Early in 1877, surveillance of the border continued as rumours of more Dakota moving north were investigated. Walsh himself took a central role in this activity. Together with the Métis scouts Morin, Léveillé, and Daniels, he kept up a constant survey of the Bad Lands that surrounded the valley of the Whitemud River. Walsh found it necessary to intercept Aboriginal people coming into Canadian territory in order to explain to them what to expect over the border. Such an occasion occurred when he approached a camp of Dakota following Four Horns, who was in search of Sitting Bull's camp. Suspicion clouded many of the initial encounters between the NWMP and the Dakota. The Aboriginal people feared that the "Red Coats" might be acting in support of the "Long Knives," and it often took considerable persuasion before such fears were alleviated. In the first encounter with Four Horns, it was eventually the reputation of Walsh himself as a fair-minded policeman that won the trust of the refugees.

In April 1877, after the arrival of Four Horns, rumours spread that Sitting Bull was approaching the border. With a handful of Mounties, as well as scouts Louis Léveillé and Gabriel Solomon, Walsh again swept the area to intercept the refugees before they reached the main body of the Dakota camp. On May 1, at the first meeting between Sitting Bull and Walsh, Sitting Bull made it clear that he did not want to fight with Canadian authorities, that he had laid down his arms at the border, and that he had only been fighting previously because he had to. Walsh told Sitting Bull, as he had told the other chiefs, Black Moon, Four Horns, and Medicine Bear, that they would be supplied with sufficient ammunition to hunt for food, and that the Dakota were subject to the Queen's law and that no breach would be tolerated. In the language of the day, they were told they could "sleep without fear." In a long exchange of speeches, Walsh was told by Chief Spotted Eagle that the Dakota in his group finally crossed the border because they feared for the lives of their women and children.

Walsh stayed in the Dakota camp the evening after the first meeting. In the morning, as he was preparing to leave, three men came riding into the camp with some horses. Among them was a Nakoda man known as White Dog, whom Gabriel Solomon recognized as a horse thief. Among the horses brought into the camp were a number that had been stolen the previous year in the Cypress Hills. Walsh walked into a large group of Dakota soldiers among whom White Dog had sought safety, and moved to arrest him. After Walsh demanded an explanation from White Dog, which he accepted — he said the horses were found astray — the Nakoda man was freed, but the police kept the horses to return them to their owners in the Cypress Hills. The incident was an indication to the Dakota of how the Mounties acted in most cases: fairly but firmly.

The presence of the Dakota in the traditional hunting territory of the Nakoda and Saulteaux produced tensions not only with the Dakota but among these other tribes as well. In May of 1877, a large group of American Assiniboine led by Crow's Dance had attempted to intimidate a group of Canadian Saulteaux to join their numbers. The Saulteaux, under Little Child, complained to Walsh about the incident, and he set off to the Nakoda camp, again outnumbered. He arrested Crow's Dance, Crooked Arm, and eleven other Nakoda. After a series of trials, Crow's Dance was given a six-month sentence, Crooked Arm two, and the eleven others were released. It was again an indication to all in the Northwest that the law was going to be enforced.

In their first encounters with the police, the Dakota who had arrived in Canada were eager to show their ties to the Crown. They related in their speeches how their history had given them a special tie to Canada. They had fought with the British in 1812, and for this reason they expected to be given sanctuary in the lands of their British allies. They expected to be protected in the land of the Great White Mother.

The Canadian government, for its part, had no intention of allowing its once-loyal allies to remain in Canada. In the summer of 1877, Assistant

Commissioner Irvine went to meet with Sitting Bull to discuss the situation. An American emissary, Father Martin Marty, head of the Roman Catholic Diocese of Dakota Territory, had come to the Dakota camp to persuade the Dakota to return to American territory, but Sitting Bull refused, having assurances — for the time being, at least — that he would be protected on Canadian soil. The efforts of Father Marty and the two other Americans with him failed enormously, and it would now fall on the shoulders of Canadian authorities to dissuade the Dakota from staying in Canada. It was clear the Long Knives and their representatives were thoroughly hated by the Dakota.

The commissioner of the NWMP, James F. Macleod, urgently advised Ottawa that the Dakota could not be allowed to remain on Canadian soil, as they were viewed with suspicion by both the Blackfoot and the Cree. The truce on the Canadian prairie between the various First Nations was uneasy at best, and the Washington and London diplomatic services should be advised of the problem at once. This advice was sent to the official diplomatic

Tatanka Iyotank, or Sitting Bull, *chief of the Hunkpapa Dakota, sought refuge east of the Cypress Hills after defeating Lt. Col. George Armstrong Custer at the Little Big Horn. For the first part of his life, Sitting Bull was known as a warrior, but by the time he arrived in Canada he had become a peacemaker, trying to protect his people* (Glenbow Archives, NA-4452-4).

services, even though the police in fact expected no trouble from the Dakota. The Mounties respected the Dakota leadership and believed the expression of peaceful intention by the chiefs. The Dakota, on the other hand, had shown great interest in remaining in Canada with the same rights accorded those Dakota who came to stay after the Minnesota Massacres of 1862. But no one wanted the Dakota in the Wood Mountain area: neither the Blackfoot, the Cree, the Nakoda, nor the Métis, neither the Mounties nor the United States Government, nor the Canadian government.

American Indian policy complicated matters further when the Nez Percé were given an ultimatum to move to their reservation voluntarily or be driven there by force. They were given thirty days from early May to comply with the order. The Nez Percé asked for more time, but it was denied them. With the same defiance exhibited by the Dakota, the Nez Percé refused to move to the new reservation, and the younger men among them organized a war party. Others decided to leave the country. By June 13, the time given by the authorities to take the new reservation had run out and war was on. The Nez Percé won some early successes against the US military forces, but by September, outnumbered and with little left to fight with, they began to move northward from the battle grounds of the Musselshell River toward the Bear's Paw Mountains. This put them within a day's journey of the Canadian border and the same safety enjoyed by the Dakota with Sitting Bull. General Miles, in pursuit of the Nez Percé, had located them in the Bear's Paw Mountains, but had been unable to defeat them. What he feared most was an attack from the Dakota in Canada, since he had suffered heavy losses against the Nez Percé.

By October, Chief Joseph recognized the futility of continued resistance and gave up. However, the requests he had made for assistance from Sitting Bull's forces had wrought havoc for Walsh and his Mountie scouts throughout the territory between Wood Mountain and the Bear's Paw Mountains. There was a constant stream of messengers to and from Sitting Bull's councilors, and the young men of the Dakota were eager to go and deliver a final defeat to the hated American forces. Walsh spent much time among the Dakota warning them that if they crossed the border to fight the Americans they would become the enemy of the Canadian authorities as well. In the end, only White Bird, with a group of ninety-eight Nez Percé men and about twenty women and children, escaped the siege imposed by General Miles in the Bear's Paw Mountains.

On October 8, rumours circulated that the Americans, having just defeated the Nez Percé, were proceeding north to attack the Dakota. The fears were unfounded; instead, the police and the Dakota discovered the straggling band of unfortunate and desperate Nez Percé under White Bird. These refugees were given sanctuary away from their hated American pursuers and were taken into the care of the Dakota. The Nez Percé who had surrendered to the Americans numbered only about 200-250. Those captured were to be taken to reservations set aside in Oklahoma, thousands of kilometres from their homelands in Oregon.

Another mission by a cleric, Father Jean Baptiste Genin, was undertaken in October 1877 to persuade the Dakota to return to American territory. Father Genin's mission, like previous attempts at persuasion, failed. Genin, however, expressed the criticism that the Dakota would not budge because they were being too well treated by the NWMP, and that their stay in Canada was becoming too comfortable for them.

Finally, it was up to an official American delegation to attempt to negotiate the return of the Dakota. The Terry Commission had been established, and was to proceed to Canadian territory and assemble at Fort Walsh to persuade, not coërce, a return of the Dakota people. The American commissioners were met at the border and escorted to Fort Walsh to begin their discussions, having telegraphed ahead in early September that they were on their way. NWMP Commissioner James F. Macleod, who had led the negotiation of Treaty 7 in Alberta, made his way to Fort Walsh, the proposed scene of the talks to be held with Sitting Bull. The officials with the NWMP were in a state of some disbelief that the Americans were sending General A. H. Terry to conduct the negotiations, since it had been Terry who, the previous year, had been commander-in-chief of the military forces sent against the Dakota.

Walsh was assigned the task of approaching Sitting Bull about attending the talks at Fort Walsh. This was not an easy job. Terry was hated not only by the Dakota but by the Nez Percé as well. He had a reputation among them for having shot innocent women and children. A. G. Lawrence, his co-commissioner, was also not well loved by the Dakota; he was with the force that took the Black Hills from them in 1875.

Sitting Bull did not want to attend any talks with Terry. He had no reason to believe any of the inducements offered after seeing his own people so recently robbed of their own homes and lands, hunted down like animals when they did not obey the arbitrary dictates of American officials. When Walsh was unable to persuade Sitting Bull, he asked his scouts, Louis Léveillé and Joseph "Blackbird" Morin, to talk to Sitting Bull in Dakota. When this failed, he asked two more Métis scouts, Antoine Ouilette and André Larivée, to speak to Sitting Bull. This final attempt at persuasion succeeded, and Sitting Bull agreed to talk to the Americans under heavy escort.

Macleod had arrived at Fort Walsh on October 1. General Terry was to be at the border five days later. For the negotiations, Walsh traveled from east of Fort Walsh with approximately twenty Dakota representatives, including, among others, Spotted Eagle, Bear's Cap, Flying Bird, Storm Bear, Iron Dog, The Crow, The-Man-that-Scatters-the-Bear, Little Knife, and Yellow Dog. Members of the delegation had already told Walsh they had no intention of surrendering to the Americans.

On October 15, in a grand ceremony at the border, Commissioner James F. Macleod met the American delegation. General Terry proceeded north to Fort Walsh, leaving three companies of cavalry behind at the border, but taking one company of infantry north as an escort. On the 16th, the cavalcade reached Fort Walsh. That evening, Sitting Bull again told Walsh he had no intention of making any concessions to Terry, and that he had been deceived so often by the Americans that he was not about to be tricked again. The position of the Americans was that the Dakota could return to the US unmolested, but that this was only on condition that they give up their guns and horses and return to their reservations. In the negotiating team for the United Sates were Terry, Lawrence, and the stenographer, Mr. Jan Stone. The party also included Jerome B. Stillson of the *New York Herald* and Charles Diehl of the *Chicago Times*.[17]

On October 17, the opposing sides sat across from one another in the officer's mess, the largest room in the fort. The Dakota representatives sat on buffalo robes on the floor, while the Americans sat at two small tables across from them. The room was crowded with reporters, NWMP representatives, interpreters, and observers. The US negotiators admitted apprehension in securing the return of Sitting Bull's Dakota to the American territory, saying they still feared the Dakota might continue hostilities against them, if given the chance.

Sitting Bull arrived at the negotiations mid-afternoon, wearing a red band of mourning for a son who had recently died. The other major negotiators for the Dakota were Spotted Eagle and The-Man-that-Scatters-the-Bear. Sitting Bull began the ceremony by taking out a pipe and lighting it. They then shook hands, and Sitting Bull requested that the tables in the room be removed, as he said they blocked his view of the American negotiators. The tables were removed.

Terry spoke to the Dakota first, saying that the commission had been established by the president to negotiate a lasting peace and an end to hostilities. The Dakota were asked to stop fighting and return to their reservations. The government extended immunity to the Dakota, and they were assured that no legal action would be taken against them for any of the previous fighting. Those who returned would be treated in the same way as those who had surrendered. Sitting Bull was assured that none of the Dakota who had surrendered and returned to the reservations had been punished, and that they had been given food and clothing. Cattle had also been purchased for the surrendering people. In return, the government expected the Dakota to give up their weapons and ammunition. Any horses deemed to be extra or for possible use in war would have to be surrendered. As well, the Dakota would have to return to their assigned reservations. Terry, perhaps the worst emissary the government could have sent, was sneered at and mocked with gestures by the Dakota as he spoke. To the Dakota, the Americans could not be serious by sending a man responsible for so many deaths.

SITTING BULL IN COUNCIL AT FORT WALSH, 1877 (*The Graphic*, New York). *The Terry Commission met with Sitting Bull to try to persuade the Dakota to return to the United States. During the meeting, Sitting Bull called the American representatives "liars," and declared that he had no intention of leaving Canada* (Glenbow Archives, NA-5091-1).

Sitting Bull rose dramatically and began by relating the history of the treaty process the Dakota had experienced with the US government. He spoke of the broken promises and the persecution. He accused Terry of telling lies, and the government of taking lands away from his people. He walked up to Commissioner Macleod and Superintendent Walsh, shaking their hands saying that he would stay in Canada. Sitting Bull's speech was a bitter denunciation of the Americans.

Others spoke as well. The-One-that-Runs-the-Ree said simply to the commissioners, "We don't like you." Another rebuked the Americans, saying, "You came here to tell lies." When Terry asked whether he was to report this refusal to return, Sitting Bull responded vigorously, telling him he did not belong in Canada, that it was not his land. Sitting Bull then left the building.

Macleod followed Sitting Bull to speak to him about the situation. He told Sitting Bull that, even though he claimed to be a British Indian, in the eyes of the Canadian authorities, he was not. The government and the NWMP considered him to be an American. They would therefore receive none of the benefits offered to Canadian treaty First Nations. Macleod warned Sitting Bull that the buffalo were increasingly scarce throughout the country, and that when they were gone his people would be reduced to destitution. Sitting Bull responded, saying they were British Indians and expressing his hatred of the Americans for stealing the lands of their ancestral home in the Black Hills:

> The Great Spirit gives us plenty of buffalo. . . . I know you will not let the Long Knives harm us. The Americans gave us sweet words; they promised us flour and cattle, but if we go back, they will kill us. . . . I could never live there again. . . . We did not wish to fight. They started it. . . . Here is nothing but good. If they liked me, as they say, why did they drive me away? Today you heard one of our women speak to the Americans — she spoke the truth. We want to raise our children and be friends with all people here. We will live in peace with the red children of the Great White Mother. . . . We are friends with you and the other officers; it was on that account that we came to meet the Americans today.[18]

Sitting Bull assured Macleod that they had absolutely no intention of going back to the border with Terry. He said they would live peaceably in the land and would obey the laws. The next day, October 18, Terry and his delegation returned to the border. The Dakota visited the fort and a feast was held.

Walsh had told the Americans that, in time, both the Nez Percé and the Dakota would be ready to return to the United States. The Mounted Police were also successful in arranging for another negotiation which, it was hoped, would lead to the return of the Dakota. On July 1, 1878, Assistant Commissioner Irvine had arranged for the Nez Percé chiefs Yellow Bull and Bald Head to meet with representatives of the American authorities at Fort Walsh. After extended negotiations between Lt. George Baird of the 5th Infantry and the Nez Percé over the fate of Chief Joseph, the Nez Percé eventually decided to stay in Canada, but these negotiations had at least made a start, and the position of each group was now better understood by their opposing numbers.

Tensions throughout 1878 were kept up with constant rumours that Louis Riel was planning to organize a great alliance of prairie Native peoples, including the Blackfoot, Dakota, Nakoda, Cree, and Métis. Walsh spent a good deal of his time in the Wood Mountain region trying to assess the truth of these rumours. Further anxiety resulted from prairie fires that had been lit just south of the 49th parallel, burning off the grass so that the buffalo were unable to move into Canadian territory. This greatly distressed the already destitute plains people, and produced numerous rumours as to who should be blamed for these fires. Some said it was Sitting Bull trying to make it appear that the Americans were responsible and, in so doing, hoping to incite other tribes to join him against the Long Knives. Others said the ultimate aim of the US army was to starve the Dakota into returning to their reserves. It appears that the fires were set neither by Sitting Bull nor by the US military, but rather by hunters trying to keep the buffalo to the south for commercial reasons. The slaughter of the great herds for the buffalo robe trade continued unabated.

The destitution caused by the diminishing resources led eventually to a weakening of the resolve of some of the Dakota on Canadian soil. In the winter of 1880, sixty lodges of Dakota under the leadership of Spotted Eagle headed for their reservation in the US, and a further twenty lodges followed the initial group. The suffering was great for those who remained. Sitting Bull's camp was plagued with disease and starvation, and often death. By the spring of 1879 the want so great in the camp of Sitting Bull that the Mounties shared their rations, and Légaré supplied the starving people with all the provisions he had left in his trading post. In spite of these circumstances, Sitting Bull and about 200 lodges in his following preferred to stay in Canada, and hoped to settle there.

Walsh maintained that even the Dakota who remained with Sitting Bull might have returned to their agencies in the US had not troops under Gen.

Nelson A. Miles, victor over the Nez Percé, continued to harass both Métis and Aboriginal hunters who ventured south of the border in search of food. Their move into US territory was motivated by starvation alone, and was not in any way undertaken to provoke hostilities.

In the summer of 1879, it was the level head of Walsh that once again calmed and blunted the aggressive intentions of US forces under General Miles. Miles had been sent to the border area because of reports of horse stealing and general lawlessness, but instead found Métis and Aboriginal hunters searching for the last of the buffalo. Walsh, who had come into US territory because of reports of conflict, explained to the American cavalry that it was need alone that caused these people to move across the border. Miles and his forces were determined to drive out all "foreign" Métis and Aboriginal people. His troops opened fire on the hunting parties and killed a number of innocent victims.

Walsh was able to secure the release of a large number of Métis whom Miles had taken into custody. He still had to deal with the Dakota, however, some of whom were anxious for revenge against the Americans for casualties among their hunters. Walsh had to warn them that they were no longer allowed to venture onto American territory, even if only to hunt. The Dakota were getting an unpleasant impression indeed of the authorities who were sending emissaries to Canada asking for the peaceable return of the Dakota to their reservations. The hand of peace was extended, but the threat of the gun was close behind.

Thus, the role of the Mounties in persuading the Dakota to return was made more difficult by the aggressive and ill-considered actions of the American military authorities. Sitting Bull's position remained firm, as he had come to despise the Americans. After the confrontation with Miles, he was said to have uttered to Walsh: "So long as there remains a gopher to eat, I will not go back."[19] The visits by missionaries such as the Reverend Mr. Marty and others did more to prevent the return of the Dakota than if they had simply been left alone, as Walsh knew full well.

Despite the tremendous workload borne by Walsh and his sensitive handling of extremely difficult situations, he was assigned a new position at Qu'Appelle, away from Wood Mountain and its responsibilities with the Dakota. Walsh was appalled by Superintendent L. N. F. Crozier, who was never able to gain the respect of the Dakota. Ironically, some officials had wanted Walsh removed from his command because he was doing too good a job in his dealings with the Dakota:

The friendship that developed between Walsh and Sitting Bull may have been the major reason for the lack of serious troubles involving the Sioux in western Canada. Walsh was, however, criticized for becoming too friendly with Sitting Bull and for failing to persuade him to return to the United States.[20]

So wrote his official biographer to explain the rather strange handling of James Walsh by his superiors. Whatever the motivation for Walsh's removal, the Dakota did ask Walsh, as a last request, to approach officials in Washington for reassurance that they would be treated fairly when and if they returned. Walsh promised to do so. The Dakota may, in fact, have felt less secure in Canada without their friend close at hand. By the end of 1880, Walsh assured the commissioner that the departure of Sitting Bull from Canada would happen shortly. He said that Sitting Bull's power had been eroded, in no small part by Walsh himself, as other chiefs had agreed to return, and members of his own camp wanted to return.

The old tactic of divide and conquer had worked once again. Throughout the winter of 1880, small groups of Dakota returned to the US, including some of the most persistent, such as the young leader Low Dog. Walsh, no longer with authority in the region, wrote:

I am in hopes that in a few weeks our territory will be rid of these troublesome intruders; we will then breathe more freely, and I for one will with all my heart say good bye to the old warrior. . . . I assure you they will be a good riddance.[21]

By the end of the winter of 1880-81, there was even more desperation in Sitting Bull's camp. They had virtually nothing to trade for food, and no prospects. Crozier was now in command, and had threatened the Dakota on a number of occasions. Feasts were held to entice the starving Dakota to leave. Crozier and Légaré made promises of provisions, horses, guns, and ammunition, if only they would leave. A small number left with Légaré in April, 1881, but most of them stayed behind, living primarily off his remaining supplies. By not providing the ammunition and assistance that were given to treaty people, the Canadian authorities were watching the Dakota make the only choice that now seemed left to them.

By May, Légaré had persuaded a second group of thirty destitute followers of Sitting Bull to head for Fort Buford in Dakota Territory. In June, the Dakota had moved to Qu'Appelle in hopes of meeting with Walsh and raising the fears of the population throughout that area. In the end, the Dakota were enticed back to Wood Mountain by the promise of food. By early July, Sitting Bull had made his last bargain for food and supplies from Légaré to tide his people over for the trip to Fort Buford. Flour, wagons, and ponies were given to the group of just over 200 left with Sitting Bull. They were met by the Americans at the border and assured of safe passage, reaching Fort Buford, Dakota Territory, on July 19.

Légaré had delivered 235 Dakota to the fort. Only a handful of the original group remained behind at Wood Mountain when Légaré returned there. Many — including the trader, Walsh, and Crozier, as well as Commissioners Macleod and Irvine — had done their best to make the Dakota leave Canada. Légaré himself was partly motivated by humanitarian concern for the Dakota and partly by the hope of compensation from the American and Canadian governments. In this hope, he was largely disappointed. He received $2,000 from the Canadian government and only $ 5,000 from the US — much less than the $46,000 he believed he was owed. The people who were the military allies of the British during their time of need in the War of 1812 were not granted asylum when the position was reversed.

Sitting Bull himself was proved right in his mistrust of the Americans, whom he despised. In 1890, at the instigation of Indian Agent James McLaughlin, he was shot by tribal police on the Standing Rock Reservation in South Dakota. Like Gabriel Dumont, Sitting Bull had toured briefly in Buffalo Bill's Wild West Show, entertaining American audiences in the years before his death. The final assessment of Sitting Bull by one biographer was that he was "the greatest Indian chief of his time, perhaps of all time, he was considered a hero by some and a savage murderer by others."[22]

The NWMP, of course, played no small role in the whole affair, and Canadians have congratulated themselves by focusing on the friendship between Walsh and Sitting Bull. It was a friendship that was betrayed. Like so many others in hierarchical organizations, Walsh could claim he was merely following orders. But Walsh seemed genuine, if not sentimental, when he wrote, in his final assessment of Sitting Bull: "He was not the bloodthirsty man reports from the prairies made him out to be. He asked for nothing but justice . . . he was not a cruel man, he was kind of heart; he was not dishonest, he was truthful."[23]

Following the diminished threat posed by Sitting Bull, the attention of the police in the Cypress Hills turned primarily to the control and surveillance of local Cree, Nakoda, and Métis populations. The Parliamentary Sessional Papers of the time suggest that more than half the arrests made concerning liquor and property were of First Nations peoples.[24] Horse stealing, and to a lesser extent cattle killing, became the Indian crimes that attracted the most NWMP attention, as they represented the elements of the prairie Aboriginal lifestyle which were the most incompatible with the emerging settler world. The ultimate goal was to restrict First Nations to the reserve lands that had been set aside for them in order to prepare the way for the flood of settlement. The police had successfully accomplished this by the late 1880s, after a severe crackdown on Aboriginal crime following the Resistance of 1885.

As the military role of patrolling the border to assert Canadian sovereignty became less significant, the need to enforce social standards and laws consistent with the hegemony of the Anglo-Canadian presence the police represented became more prominent. The police themselves saw their role as one of civilizing the territory. The implication in their belief that they represented those who were legitimately bringing civilization to the West left no doubt about who they thought comprised the "savage" half of the civilization-savagery question.

In the 1870s, the Métis in the Cypress Hills were also looking for a treaty. The name Alexis Labombarde appears, among others, on an 1878 petition signed by the "Half-Breeds Living in the Vicinity of Cypress Hills" sent to the Council of the North-West Territories. The Métis in the Cypress Hills hoped for a reserve like those established for the Aboriginal nations as part of Treaty 6.[25] The government disregarded the petition. Alexis had already received scrip worth 160 acres or $160 of Dominion land as a Métis head of family, part of the Canadian government's settlement with the Métis in Manitoba after 1870. In the late 1870s and early 1880s, Alexis and his family wintered, with other hunters and freighters, fifty-one kilometres east of the Hudson's Bay Company post at Racette Crossing.[26] Like Louis Riel, the Lambombardes could be found "across the line" in this period, and, like him, by 1885 they were living along the south branch of the Saskatchewan River at Batoche.[27] Alexis served as Riel's interpreter during the Resistance of 1885. He was arrested after the fall of Batoche and charged with "treason felony." Tried in Regina on August 12, 1885, he pleaded guilty, and was conditionally discharged on his own recognizance to appear for sentencing, if the Crown should see fit.[28] Alexis and Madame Labombarde, Nancy, both made claims with the North-West Rebellion Scrip Commission. There was a delay in Alexis's claim because of his "rebel" status. On February 25, 1890, it was recommended he receive $160 in scrip, but Nancy's claim was disallowed.[29]

CHAPTER SEVEN

The Nakoda

The Nakoda and the Hills

The Nakoda, also known as the Assiniboine, are among the oldest nations known to have inhabited the Great Plains or prairie environment. The Souian-speaking Nakoda were given the name "Assiniboine" by the neighbouring Algonquian tribes, referring to them as "those who cook with stones." In the Nakoda language, their name is an ancient word, the root of the word "peace," meaning "the friendly people." Jesuits observed the Nakoda cooking with stones and recorded this name in their journals. The Nakoda say this method of cooking was only used when they were travelling. This method of cooking with heated stones in a buffalo bladder was developed so that, if threatened by an enemy, the food could be gathered up quickly and not left behind.

Until the seventeenth century, the Nakoda lived peacefully among the Lakota, or Sioux, nations now located in present-day Minnesota and Dakota territory. By the eighteenth century, the Nakoda had separated from the Lakota bands and occupied territory to the north and west. One group of Lakota, better known as the Stoney, came furthest west, settling on the edge of the Rockies and taking a reserve in the area of Morley, Alberta. Nakoda elders giving evidence in the United States Court of Federal Claims consistently described the traditional territory of their people as stretching across the central Great Plains of both Canada and the United States.[1] The main tribes of the Nakoda remained in an area bounded on the east by the Lake of the Woods, on the north by the North Saskatchewan River, on the west by the Rocky

Mountain foothills, and on the south by the Missouri and Yellowstone rivers. In these prairie and parkland environments, they followed seasonal cycles based on the movements of the buffalo herds and the maturation of berries and wild vegetables throughout their territory; they also harvested wild rice in the regions southeast of Lake Winnipeg.[2]

The Nakoda traded with their neighbours, such as the Mandan, for agricultural goods, and were active in the fur trade from the seventeenth century through to its decline at the end of the nineteenth century. The Nakoda were expert horsemen, and on the plains they raised horses for their own use and for trade. They negotiated a variety of alliances over the years with the neighbouring nations of the Cree, Dakota, Blackfoot, Lakota, Gros Ventre, Crow, Mandan, and Hidatsa.[3] In the early nineteenth century, before being devastated by smallpox, they were thought to have numbered 80,000, and some estimates suggest their numbers were much higher.[4]

Like other plains people, the Nakoda developed a complex system of societies that defined their social relations, government, and religious life. Many of these social events, such as the Grass Dance (pow-pow) and Sun Dance or Medicine Lodge Dance (for the Nakoda) have remained active to the present day. Nakoda societies have remained active, in spite of restrictions imposed by the *Indian Act*. Indeed, the Nakoda maintain their own forms of democracy and decision-making alongside government-sanctioned forms of administration. The culture and social life of the Nakoda have been observed and described over the years by many European travellers, traders, and missionaries, including Father Pierre-Jean De Smet, Charles Larpenteur, George Catlin, the Earl of Southesk, Reverend Robert Rundle, Viscount Milton, Lord Cheadle, Alexander Henry, and La Vérendrye.

A rich record of Nakoda history and culture was written in the late nineteenth and early twentieth centuries by historian Dan Kennedy.[5] Kennedy was educated at St. Boniface College, and published much about Nakoda history and culture. The life Kennedy describes shows that many social and religious practices remained vibrant, even through times of starvation, relocation, and disease. In particular, he provides us with Eashappie's first-hand account of the Cypress Hills Massacre of 1873, when a group of Nakoda were attacked by American wolfers. The Cypress Hills had long been an important spiritual place for the Nakoda, a place where they sought refuge in winter and where they hunted the abundant game in the hills.

The Cypress Hills remain significant to the Nakoda, who refer to them as *Wazi-ka,* "the place where the land gets rough or broken," and also "a warm place in the north that is an island by itself." Early European travellers across the Great Plains, such as Edwin Denig and George Catlin, described the territory of the Nakoda as including the Cypress Hills. Later observers, such as Isaac Cowie, Norbert Welsh, and Louis Goulet, recorded the presence of the Nakoda as hunters and traders in the Cypress Hills. Nakoda elders, who gave evidence concerning the Fort Laramie Treaty of 1851 in the United States Court of Federal Claims in 1929, virtually all described the Cypress Hills as a major landmark within the territory they traditionally traversed. These Nakoda remember Long Lodge as a signatory of Redstone's Treaty in 1866, and as an influential and powerful chief among the Nakoda in the mid to late 1880s.[6] Elders from Carry the Kettle reserve (located south of Sintaluta, Sask., some 87 kilometres east of Regina) describe the Cypress Hills as one of the places most sacred to their people, and as a place of great economic importance to them. The lodgepole pine was a critical resource, used for horse and dog travois and also for tipi poles. Buffalo crossing over and between the hills were a major source of food for the Nakoda, but as the buffalo declined, the deer, elk, and antelope become important sources of meat. The berries that grew in and around the Cypress Hills were an important part of the Nakoda diet as well, and their seasonal cycle included movements to areas where large concentrations of berries and buds could be found, including choke cherries, saskatoons, raspberries, rosebuds, bull berries, gooseberries, and currants. Other fruits were also picked to be eaten fresh or dried. Turnips, wild onion, and wild rhubarb could also be found, along with a variety of wild hops. The Nakoda also collected many plants and herbs for medicinal purposes.

The spiritual nature of the Cypress Hills is perhaps of greatest significance for the Nakoda. Elders remember that the hills were a major burial site for their ancestors. Stone markers from Nakoda camps dating back hundreds of years can be found there, and many important cultural events have occurred in the hills over hundreds of years.

The Cypress Hills was traditionally the location of one of the most sacred ceremonies of the Nakoda, the Medicine Lodge Dance, which was held following the first thunder in spring. Elders still visit the site of this historical ceremony, as many elders from Carry the Kettle reserve still visit the Cypress Hills for spiritual renewal. It was not only the location of the Medicine Lodge Dance, but also a vision quest site for the youth and holy men who would seek solitude in the hills while fasting. Many elders feel that they lost much of their cultural memory and ceremony when they were removed from the hills. Stories that can be told only in particular places, as well as ceremonies that are attached to particular environments, are being lost. The laws of sacred societies often restrict who can tell stories or initiate ceremonies, and they can also restrict the place where ceremonies can take place or where stories can be told. The Nakoda have endured emotional, spiritual, and psychological trauma by being removed so far from the burial site of their ancestors and from this cultural homeland.[7]

The Nakoda and Treaty 4

On September 4, 1874, the Crown and the First Nations of the Cree, Saulteaux, and "other Indians" signed Treaty 4,[8] an agreement that would allow settlers on the lands occupied by these nations in return for the "bounty and benevolence" of Her Majesty. Treaty 4 covered most of the southern Canadian prairies, including all of the Cypress Hills.

Disagreement remains between Canada and the other signatories over the meaning of the treaty. Canada has characterized it as a land surrender, whereas First Nations say they essentially agreed to share the land with newcomers, and that there would be "peace and good-will" between the First Nations and Her Majesty. Canada has traditionally emphasized that the treaties were narrowly legal and primarily land surrenders, while First Nations claim that the treaties were more broadly peace treaties that emphasized sharing the land with assurances from the Crown that they would be able to continue their way of life. First Nations say that the written text contains wording that was never discussed with them, and that the full spirit and intent of the treaty is not represented by the text. They say the treaty established a relationship and meant that they were to benefit from the development of their lands in the same way the settlers and newcomers were to benefit. They were promised that they could count on the "bounty and benevolence" of the Crown in return for allowing newcomers to settle among them. They were told that they could take land in their traditional territories, but the nature of the reserves that were eventually surveyed for them was never fully explained, nor were the many restrictions of the *Indian Act*.[9] Major promises contained in the written text include mutual obligations regarding peace and good-will; education through the maintenance of schools and provision for teaching; the pursuit of hunting and fishing as it existed at the time of the treaty, except on settled land and contingent on government regulation; $750 per year for powder, shot, bale, and twine; reserve land of one section per family of five; assistance with agriculture, including seed to plant wheat, barley, oats, and potatoes on land that had been broken, as well as ploughs and harrows, carpenter's tools, hand saws, augers, files, and a grindstone; also oxen, bulls, and cows; and annuity payments.

The adhesion to Treaty 4, signed by the Nakoda in 1877, was agreed to at a time of great tension in Canada's North-West. After the Cypress Hills Massacre in 1873, the North West Mounted Police had been dispatched to bring order to the border areas of Canada's prairie territory. The presence of Sitting Bull's Lakota and Chief Joesph's Nez Percé on Canadian territory presented Canada with the possibility of an international incident should they use Canada as a base from which to make raids into US territory, perhaps even provoking US forces to cross the border into Canada. It was therefore important for Canadian officials to conclude treaties with as many Canadian First Nations as possible in order to break up large concentrations of dissatisfied people. It has been suggested that the threat of an international crisis led to the government making unrealistic or insincere promises to those tribes who had not yet taken treaty. The negotiation of Treaty 7, also in September 1877, was an occasion in which the government could not afford to have the process break down.

It has been argued, for example, that at Treaty 7 the issue of land surrender might not have been raised out of fear that the Blackfoot Confederacy would not agree to such a provision. Instead, the government made extravagant commitments in order to secure an agreement. Like the Nakoda elders, the Treaty 7 signatories believed they had signed a peace treaty that would allow newcomers to share the land in return for the "bounty and benevolence of the Queen."

Nakoda elders insist that the treaty was much more than a narrow legal agreement that featured the extinguishment of legal title to the land. In the 1980s Walter Gordon, a respected elder and Nakoda historian, interviewed Nakoda elders to record their understanding of the treaty they had made with the Crown. The four elders represented by this document were Charles Ryder, Jr., Lena Eashappie, Hector Eashappie, and George Rider, all highly respected members of their community.[10]

What was emphasized first and foremost was the sacredness of the treaty that was made with Canada. Pipes smoked at important events sealed the occasion. The solemn nature of the agreement, arrived at in good faith, is preserved by the pipe, which is smoked to seal major decisions. The sacredness of the treaty was sealed with the promise that it would never be broken. In 1881, Man Who Took the Coat clearly told government officials that he could not leave the Cypress Hills reserve because of the promise that he had made with the Queen's representatives when he agreed to take a reserve. Man Who Took the Coat considered this agreement as one that could not be broken, and, even though government officials were asking him to leave, it is clear that he did not want to break the promises he had made solemn with the smoking of the pipe when he took his reserve.[11]

The treaty was a peace treaty by which both sides agreed no longer to go to war, and to maintain law and order. Both sides agreed to respect laws that would apply both to Canada and First Nations. The Nakoda remembered being promised that they could continue to pursue hunting, fishing, and trapping, as they always had. They were promised that they could continue to harvest in their traditional territories root crops, berries, timber for lodges, maple trees for sugar, lakes for wild rice, and meadows for medicinal plants and herbs. There was a sacred understanding that the Nakoda could continue to pursue their way of life. The elders also remember that promises were made to help their people as the buffalo disappeared. They were promised assistance in agriculture through the appointment of farm instructors, and education through the appointment of teachers. They were promised ammunition and fishing nets, annuity payments, salaries, uniforms, and freedom from taxes. The Nakoda promised, in turn, to use their warriors as policemen, to obey the laws, and "never to alienate any of their lands and any of their resources." The land and resources were to be preserved for future generations of their people. The Nakoda solemnly agreed that they would never abandon their reserves.

They agreed to the provisions of Treaty 4, in the words of the adhesion, "as if we ourselves and the band which we represent had been originally contracting parties thereto and had been present and attached our signatures to the said treaty."[12] The agents of the treaty commissioners who negotiated the adhesion were all members of the NWMP and included Major James Walsh and sub-inspectors J. H. McIllree and Percy Neale. This adhesion was arrived at in the traditional territory of the Nakoda, the Cypress Hills, the area in which they wished to take their reserve.

The Cypress Hills Reserve, 1879-82

In 1879, after consulting with officers of the Crown and in compliance with Treaty 4, the Nakoda who signed the 1877 adhesion chose a reserve in the Cypress Hills. On being advised of their intentions, Commissioner Edgar Dewdney sent farm instructor J. J. English to the Cypress Hills to discuss the location with Chief Man Who Took the Coat. They agreed that a survey of land immediately to the north and west of the hills would be undertaken the following year. As stipulated in the treaty, the land was deemed suitable for agriculture. In 1880, after consultation with the chiefs of the Nakoda bands, A. P. Patrick surveyed a reserve for Man Who Took the Coat and Long Lodge. The size of the reserve surveyed was 340 square miles.[13] The Nakoda believed they had a legally constituted reserve after Patrick completed the survey in 1880. It was in a place that had long been economically and spiritually important to the Nakoda, where many of the their ancestors were buried, and it was the site of their Medicine Lodge Dance.

Economically, it made sense for the Nakoda to establish their reserve in an area they knew to have both abundant game and the plants necessary for their diet and for medicines. They possessed extensive knowledge of the indigenous game, and the area would be an ideal environment to begin farming, since the game could help sustain their people if crops failed. Their knowledge of rainfall and frost patterns would give them the kind of information necessary to establish successful farming operations. Patrick agreed that the land would be ideal for farming.

The reserves were never intended to be merely places of confinement; they were to become places where agricultural economies were to replace the nomadic life of the buffalo hunt. The Nakoda were provided with a farm instructor, J. J. English, as soon as their reserve was chosen. They planted crops in the first year of their residency, even though all the supplies that had been promised did not arrive as expected. As was the case on prairie reserves across the West, there were some successes and some failures in the first years of working the land. Both Aboriginal and non-Aboriginal farmers struggled with the environment, learning the best techniques of farming the prairie successfully. Not all band members took to agriculture; some continued to hunt — primarily out of necessity, since agriculture did not produce enough food to ward off starvation. As was the case on most prairie reserves, even those who farmed had to hunt to complement the crops they harvested.

The farm of J. J. English is a clear illustration of Canada's Indian policy. English's farm was designated as a training ground for the home farm plan established in 1879 by the federal government to educate Aboriginal farmers. The Home Farm Plan was a central feature of Canada's agricultural policy, and one of a number of initiatives directed toward making reserve farmers self-sufficient. It was also partially implemented because of the starvation crisis that existed in the North-West by the late 1870s.

The historical record, especially the reports from government agents and the NWMP, indicates that farming on the Nakoda reserve in the early years was successful. A crop was planted in the first year, and Commissioner Dewdney, reporting on the farming operations in Treaty 4 generally, wrote that there was "very satisfactory progress" on many reserves, and that many reserve farmers were turning out to be "good ploughmen, mowers, and, in fact, good useful farm hands."[14] The home farm established by J. J. English along Maple Creek was cited in particular as being a success. English, who was from Omenee, Ontario, worked well with the Nakoda farmers and was able to establish an atmosphere of trust with them. After two seasons, the Inspector of Indian Agencies, T. P. Wadsworth, wrote to Assistant Commissioner Lawrence Vankoughnet that the Nakoda farm had produced two good crops; indeed, Wadsworth boasted that the farm had produced a yield of wheat "equal to any in the Territories prov[ing] that it is adapted for agriculture."[15] Also in 1881, Indian Agent Cecil Denny wrote that the Nakoda farm was doing well, having produced 70,000 lbs. of potatoes and good grain crops as well.[16] Even in the last year of its existence, the produce from the Nakoda farm was transported to Fort Walsh and distributed to the sick and starving by the NWMP. The food produced by the Nakoda on English's home farm might well have been enough to feed themselves, had it not been diverted to other, non-treaty groups camped in the Cypress Hills.

Letters written by English to his hometown newspaper, *The Omenee Herald*, documented the early successes of agriculture on the reserve. English described his travel to the reserve in 1880 and its location "at the head of Cypress Mountain, a distance of 18 miles from the Fort" [Fort Walsh]. He went on to describe the praise he received from the Assistant Commissioner for the progress being made on the reserve, and he described the agricultural activity on the reserve in 1880: "have thirty acres under crop, broken this Spring with one team, out of sod. The crop consists of six acres of wheat, eight of potatoes, seven of oats, and seven of barley, with two acres of turnips and carrots and about two of garden vegetables." English stated that his work included distributing rations to "about eight hundred Indians" each morning, consisting of a half pound of flour and a half pound of beef for each family member: "the cattle are driven up from the Government herd at the Fort, and killed on the reservation." It is clear from English's reports that many Nakoda were farming: "I have forty Indians at work, for which they receive extra rations. They work well and I have very little trouble with them. They are very kind to me and often make me presents."[17]

In spite of the reports of successful farming on the Nakoda reserve by Indian Agents and the NWMP, Commissioner Dewdney began to insist that farming in the Cypress Hills was proving futile. In one report to the Superintendent General of Indian Affairs (S.G.I.A.), John A. Macdonald, Dewdney contradicted the attached report of his Indian agent, claiming, "The soil, moreover in the vicinity [of the Nakoda reserve] being for the most part ill-adapted for agriculture, it has been found impossible to provide Indians able to work with employment in return for the food given them, as is done in the more fertile districts."[18] Later, in August, 1881, Indian Inspector T. P. Wadsworth also changed his mind, contradicting his earlier, positive assessments: "I do not look upon our only Farm in this section as a very great success and we would be gainers by not continuing it."[19] By the summer of 1881, it appears that Dewdney's intention of clearing the Cypress Hills of non-treaty bands had widened to include treaty Indians of the Nakoda bands of Man Who Took the Coat and Long Lodge. Reports describing successful farming operations exist side by side with reports that claim farming in the Cypress Hills was a disaster.[20] It is clear that, if Dewdney was to be successful in removing all tribes from the Cypress Hills, he could not acknowledge

NWMP OFFICER JAMES H. SCHOFIELD *and his horse at Fort Walsh, June, 1878* (photo by George Anderton, Glenbow Archives NA-1602-5).

a successful farming operation there. By the summer of 1881, government agents in the Cypress Hills began to echo Dewdney's claims that farming in the Cypress Hills was proving impossible. Dewdney either ignored the many favourable reports of farming or misrepresented and contradicted them.

Historian Sarah Carter, analyzing the home farm plan across the prairies, found that it was a mixed success, owing in part to poor instructors, poor supplies, and an environment untested for agriculture. Carter did find, however, that the home farms in the Cypress Hills were promising from the outset. In the second year, it was reported that 115 acres of wheat, oats, turnips, and potatoes were planted. Working relations between farm instructors John Setter and J. J. English and reserve farmers in the Cypress Hills were reported to be exceptional:

> Some of the Indians were reported to be working at their farms remarkably well; they took considerable pride in their gardens and were annoyed that more seed was not available. A number planted wheat for themselves, and the agent recommended that a portable grist mill be supplied, as he believed that if the Indians could grind their grain, many more could be induced to break up land for the following year. The agent was confident that the Indians could be self-sustaining in another year.[21]

Carter continued:

> Despite the fact that John Setter's home farm in the Cypress Hills proved to be one of the great successes of the program, it as well as J. J. English's farm, was closed because of the decision in the winter of 1881-82 that all Indians in the Cypress Hills be moved north or east.[22]

It is clear that farming — and, later, ranching — were compatible with the climate and environment of the Cypress Hills. But Dewdney knowingly misrepresented what was evident to observers of these early farming operations. When he called the Cypress Hills unsuitable for agriculture, he was contradicting reports that came across his own desk.

Nakoda elders believed they had both a legal and a *de facto* reserve in the Cypress Hills. They remembered that many band members willingly undertook farming, and that they did not want to leave this reserve. Both Canada and the NWMP broke treaty promises that they would protect the Nakoda and assist them to realize the "bounty" of the land and the "benevolence" of the Crown.

The Removal of the Nakoda from the Cypress Hills

The success rate of the crops in the first two years was better than farming on most reserves as Aboriginal farmers experimented with what could be grown. There was also active participation in farming from many of the reserve residents. But in 1881 the Canadian government became concerned about the large number of people in the Cypress Hills, and changed its mind about allowing reserves there, as had been promised in the treaty. The decision that no reserves were to be allowed in the Cypress Hills was taken unilaterally, without consultation or agreement from the Nakoda who were already on reserve. Having arbitrarily decided that the failure of agriculture was one reason reserves could not be maintained in the Cypress Hills, the government began to talk to chiefs individually to try to persuade them to leave the hills for the Qu'appelle area. The chiefs were never together during these talks, but were told individually that the others had agreed to move. Sick and starving Nakodas were given minimal rations in order to pressure them to move.

Historian John Tobias has documented Indian Commissioner Edgar Dewdney's decision to remove all Aboriginal tribes from the Cypress Hills. Dewdney expanded the Mounted Police force at the same time he was planning to close Fort Walsh, where rations for starving people were distributed. He "hoped that starvation would drive them from the Fort Walsh area."[23] Acting contrary to the provisions of Treaties 4 and 6, in which it was clear that reserves could be established anywhere within the traditional territory of the bands, Dewdney used the "hunger crisis" — a crisis he had helped to create — to remove tribes from the Cypress Hills.

By the summer of 1881, the correspondence among government officials made it clear that neither treaty nor non-treaty Indians would be allowed to remain in the Cypress Hills. Throughout the late 1870s and early 1880s, an elaborate paper trail was created documenting the flow of information from the Cypress Hills to the regional offices of Indian Affairs in Regina and Winnipeg and to headquarters in Ottawa. Both the NWMP and local Indian agents began a campaign to persuade the Nakoda to leave the hills. In spite of the persistence of the campaign, and promises of more rations on agreeing to move, the Nakoda maintained that they did not want to leave.

On five occasions, agents reported to Dewdney their great disappointment at their failure to make headway with the Nakoda. Before 1881, Dewdney had already written to Prime Minister Macdonald that "it cannot be expected that either the Blackfoot or Assiniboines can be induced to leave their own territory."[24] In July, 1881, Wadsworth wrote to Dewdney that he was making a great effort to persuade the Nakoda to leave: "Upon my return I again held a meeting with the Assiniboines and told them I could not consent to them taking a reservation in this part of the country, and I was prepared to give them a good one at either the Touchwood Hills, Qu'appelle or Crooked Lakes."[25] Again in late July, Assistant Indian Commissioner Galt wrote to Dewdney that the Nakoda refused to co-operate with attempts to relocate them. In October, 1881, Vankoughnet wrote that the fifty-three remaining Nakoda could be persuaded to leave their reserve.[26] On another occasion, in January, 1882, Dewdney was told by Indian Agent Cecil Denny that, "as yet I have no decided answer from the Assiniboines who do not like to leave their country."[27] In February 1882, Indian Agent McIllree wrote:

They listened to my proposition and to all the reasons I gave why the Government thought it better for them to move from here. They promised to answer me in a day or two. Two days later they all turned up again and each made a speech and they all agreed in this, that they wanted to remain in this section of the country and settle permanently on Maple Creek Reserve. Their chief arguments against moving were that they were brought up in this country, that although they had given up their country to the Queen who had promised them a Reserve in whatever part of the country they liked to pick out, that they did not like the northern country or the Indians living there and hoped that the Government would allow them to remain here. The Man That Took the Coat asked me to tell you that this was the first time he had ever refused to do as the Queen asked him, but he said he loved the country and wanted to remain here and hoped the government would not be angry with him.[28]

Thus, up to the winter of 1882, it was obvious to government officials that the Nakoda in the Cypress Hills had no intention of leaving. They had smoked the pipe when they agreed to live in the Cypress Hills, and for them this was a sacred agreement. Yet Dewdney insisted that the Nakoda were willing to leave. Both he and Wadsworth claimed the Nakoda had agreed to go, even as they were receiving reports to the contrary. When the Nakoda finally did move, it was because they had been left in such a state of destitution that they had no option but to go wherever they were promised food. At no time in the documentary record is there any report of any surrender vote being taken.

Nakoda elders say that no such vote was ever taken, and that they did not voluntarily leave their reserve.[29] There is no evidence that the Nakoda voluntarily agreed to go, except for Dewdney's assertions that they had done so. It is clear that he had a vested interest in saying that the Indians were leaving the Cypress Hills voluntarily, but the historical record shows that there was a complete absence of consent. The Nakoda were escorted by the NWMP to Indian Head in what could only be characterized as a military escort.

Canada showed little humanitarian concern for the suffering of the Nakoda. Their removal from the Cypress Hills was not unlike the removal of the Cherokee in 1838 from their eastern homelands to Oklahoma, which has become known as the "Trail of Tears." As in the American example, the Canadian government supplied inadequate transportation and minimal rations. Many who made the journey were severely weakened, and a number died. Even so, the Nakoda attempted to return to the Cypress Hills the same year; they were rounded up and forced to return to Indian Head.

By July of 1881, the policy to remove all bands from the Cypress Hills had been clearly defined.[30] In August of 1881, Wadsworth wrote to Dewdney that it would be necessary to abandon Fort Walsh and also quit the home farms in order to achieve the complete removal of all tribes.[31] Wadsworth wrote that, without the rations that were being distributed out of Fort Walsh, none of the bands would remain. He agreed with the policy of reducing rations to a minimum to persuade the Indians to leave. He further pointed out that, by abandoning the home farms along with the police fort, the remaining bands would be vulnerable to raids from the Blackfoot Confederacy to the west. He reiterated his belief that, if Canadian authority left the area, the remaining bands would be too frightened to stay. It is clear that Dewdney agreed with Wadsworth, and he recommended the abandonment of Fort Walsh and the home farms in the Cypress Hills. Both these actions were in clear breach of Treaty 4. They were also in breach of the fiduciary obligations of the Crown to maintain law and order and give protection to tribes. The presence of the NWMP was to prevent old enemies from going to war. Creating a vacuum of authority was thus a direct violation of the treaty right to law and order.

Reduced rations, altering the diet, and even advocating starvation were the main tactics the government adopted to achieve full removal of the tribes from the Cypress Hills. By the summer of 1881, only half-rations were to be distributed among the tribes remaining in the hills. There was resistance from at least one Indian Agent, who protested that the reduction would result in "restless Indians . . . at this critical period."[32] Protests from the police were few, however, and compliance emerged as the norm. As Indian Agent Cecil Denny reported in November, 1881, "Everything going well here, I am doing my best to keep down the ration list, feeding only those who I find cannot do so for themselves."[33] Denny was alarmed by the number of bands returning from the buffalo hunt in a state of starvation, yet he reported that he was providing no rations but was, instead, giving the men ammunition so they could hunt for themselves.[34]

Indian Affairs officials hoped to encourage the removal of First Nations from the Cypress Hills by changing their meat rations from fresh beef to bacon. In May 1881, Assistant Indian Commissioner E. J. Galt had recommended to Prime Minister John A. Macdonald that this would be a cost-saving measure. Galt went on to point out that the change in diet would be repugnant to the bands: "Another feature in feeding bacon which should not be lost sight of is that the Indians are not as fond of it as beef, besides which it is more easily handled."[35]

A year later, in May 1882, Colonel Irvine wrote that, "I have fully determined to starve them out if they remain here."[36] By that time, most tribes in the Cypress Hills were in a desperate state, and it was clear that, if the Nakoda were to survive, they would have to go where they would be given rations. According to the elders, it was for this reason that they finally followed the government officials to Indian Head and the reserve that had been created for them. Nakoda elders said they felt they were being escorted like cattle.[37]

There is no evidence that a proper surrender of the Cypress Hills reserve was ever executed. If sacred land had been surrendered, the Nakoda would certainly have remembered the occasion and commemorated it with a ceremony. The government itself acknowledged that such removals were objectionable, yet the removal of the Nakoda took place with the full knowledge of senior government officials.[38]

The Indian Head Reserve

The Nakoda bands of Long Lodge and Man Who Took the Coat were removed to a reserve at Indian Head that had been chosen by the Cree chief, Piapot. The Nakoda did not like their new location, since it did not have adequate fishing, large game, or timber for shelter. They had been promised a large reserve, but the new survey was only 220 square miles — much smaller than the Cypress Hills reserve of 340. Also, they did not like the Hurricane Hills on the reserve, which contained the skulls of hundreds of Cree who had died during an epidemic in the 1840s.

The new Indian Agent on the Indian Head reserve was Allan McDonald, who immediately began to work with the Nakoda to plough land and plant potatoes. McDonald wrote in June that the Nakoda who arrived with chiefs Long Lodge and Man Who Took the Coat numbered ninety-seven and 157, respectively. It was obvious, he wrote, that the Nakoda did not want to be there: "That signs of discontent and expression of unwillingness to go to their Reserve had been noticed and gleaned there is no denying." He went on to report that many Nakoda were grieving the deaths of their people who had died along the route, and "of course you are fully acquainted with the veneration and love that Indians all exhibit towards the spot where their parents or relatives lie buried, so there is some excuse for the Long Lodge party not appearing as contented as might be desired by us."[39]

A month after the Indian Head reserve was settled, both Cree and Nakoda complained that they were starving and dying. According to McDonald, reserve residents complained that the food they were given was killing them:

> that from childhood they have become accustomed to fresh meat and not bacon, that several of them had died from the change of diet. That he [Piapot] had heard of Indians dying of starvation in this district and that he did not wish his people to go off that way.[40]

He confirmed complaints from Piapot, Long Lodge, and Man Who Took the Coat, reporting that the change in diet had been "hurtful." He then described the sickness: "there is no doubt that an alarming amount of sickness of the type of Diarrhea has been prevailing among the Nakoda and which there is also no doubt has arisen from the change from fresh meat diet to that of bacon."[41] McDonald begged the department to issue fresh meat, and warned that, if this were not done, the bands would return to the Cypress Hills. He described the morale on the reserve as desperately low. Starvation and death surrounded him:

> Added to this is the suicide of an old man of Piepot's [sic] band whose granddaughter had died two days ago from Diarrhea. The old man finding himself deserted as it were pushed a sharp stick down his throat from which resulted his death. It is needless for me to point out to you the demoralizing effect of deaths in a new camp, especially where excuses for discontent are eagerly sought after.[42]

Local officials as well as Dewdney were concerned that the Cree and Nakoda would not stay on their reserve unless promises made to them could be kept and supplies were provided to them immediately. Already in August 1882, eighteen lodges of Long Lodge's band had left for the Cypress Hills.[43] In October, NWMP scout and interpreter Peter Hourie reported that Piapot and the Nakoda were back at Fort Walsh, hoping to get fresh meat instead of the bacon that was making them sick. Hourie further reported: "They are trying hard to get their payments here and I think they will gain their point, for if they are not treated with and fed they will freeze and starve to death."[44] He reiterated that all members of Man That Took the Coat's band were on their way to Fort Walsh in search of fresh meat. Comptroller Fred White, who was travelling through the North-West at the time, was appalled by the situation he found at Fort Walsh:

> I arrived here on the night of the 14th and since then have devoted myself closely to the Indian situation. There are about 260 lodges in this vicinity, and a more wretched half starved camp could not be imagined. The provisions issued to them have averaged about 4 oz. of flour and 2 oz. of dried meat per day. . . . They are huddled together two or three families to a lodge, the lodges are old and dilapidated and the women and children are suffering from want of food and clothing, in fact some children are quite naked. It has snowed every day since I arrived and unless something is done for them without delay the old people and the young children who are now lying prostrate from starvation must succumb.[45]

Surgeon Augustus Jukes, who was travelling with White, also observed and reported on the deplorable conditions:

> They are literally in a starving condition and destitute of the commonest necessaries of life. . . . their clothing for the most part miserable and scanty in the extreme, I saw little children at this inclement season, snow having fallen who had scarcely rags to cover them. Of food they possessed little or none, some were represented to me as absolutely starving. . . . it would be difficult to exaggerate their extreme wretchedness and need, or urgent necessity which exists for some prompt and sufficient provision being made for them by the Government.[46]

Jukes warned that, without immediate action, the consequences would be "disastrous and even appalling." But Commissioner Dewdney did not want to feed any Indians at Fort Walsh. If necessary, he told Irvine, they should be sent to Swift Current and fed there. He indicated to Irvine that the people should be told that they had brought the suffering on themselves, and that no food should be given to them unless it were absolutely necessary, as "the longer they continue to act against the wishes of the Government the more wretched will they become."[47] The advice to send the Nakoda many kilome-

BLACK EYES AND STABBED MANY TIMES. *Stabbed Many Times is a legendary warrior woman among the Nakoda. It is told that she had a vision of a battle between the Nakoda and the Blackfoot. In the vision, she fought the Blackfoot and was wounded during the battle. She saw herself being healed by lying on a bed of cedar branches. After actually being wounded, she was able to heal herself by following her vision. The Nakoda honoured her bravery in battle by making her the first woman to dance during a pow wow. Her dress had the shape of a hand drawn on it and red paint splattered across the hand representing the blood shed from war wounds* (courtesy Elsie Koochicum).

tres away to Swift Current was chilling, in light of the fact that they were destitute and had had their horses stolen by raiding Blackfoot.

Many Cree, Saulteaux, and Nakoda at the fort were, ironically, still being fed with supplies from the home farm of J. J. English, but they were unable to hunt without horses, so the ammunition supplied them was virtually useless.[48] Some agents were appalled by Dewdney's insistence on meagre rations. Inspector Frank Norman of the NWMP wrote in December 1882:

> To reduce the present allowance of food to these Indians in my opinion cannot possibly be done as they are merely existing on the allowance I am at present giving them. There is a great deal of misery in all the camps owing to the old women and children being housed in wretched cotton lodges, which are no protection whatever in cold weather, their clothing is poor and the only means they have to living, is the small issue of food they are presently receiving from the Government.[49]

The Aboriginal groups in the Cypress Hills endured a horrific winter. Problems were compounded by supplies that were unable to reach Fort Walsh because of the deep snow.[50] By the following spring, the government attempted to move the Nakoda who were in terrible physical condition. They were brought to Maple Creek and loaded onto railway flat-cars.[51] Barely en route, the cars overturned, injuring a number of people. Elder Kay Thompson remembered that many Nakoda bore scars from when the train crashed, and that many elders believed the derailment had been planned; they felt they were being loaded onto the trains like cattle to the slaughter. They refused to ride the train any further and walked the remainder of the journey to Indian Head; once more, a number died along the way. Nakoda elders say they buried the dead at Maple Creek, Gull Lake, and present-day Pilot Mound.[52]

Demoralized after a second removal from their ancient home, the Nakoda were physically weakened and suffering badly. The chiefs continued to complain about the lack of fresh running water on the reserve, and the lack of fresh meat. In 1884, Dr. O. G. Edwards reported continuing sickness and death from malnutrition on the Indian Head reserve.[53] He reported bronchial disease and people dying of consumption. He diagnosed the deaths as resulting from a form of scurvy caused by the exclusive consumption of salt foods.[54] In May 1884, Edwards reported that seventy-five people had died on the reserve and he did not have enough medicine to treat all those who needed it. He blamed the deaths on the inadequate diet, and recommended fresh meat and rice be given immediately:

> Many of those who have died this winter had died from absolute starvation. They were ill and could not eat the bacon and flour and having nothing else died. The only proper treatment of this disease on land or sea is fresh food and vegetables and unless this policy is pursued in the case of these Indians the disease will spread.[55]

The authorities did not act on this disturbing information.

Both the Nakoda and the Cree at Indian Head continued to express their dissatisfaction. Piapot asked for a new reserve because of sickness on the existing one, and was eventually granted a reserve in the Qu'appelle Valley in 1885.[56] Similar requests were denied the Nakoda, and the Indian Head reserve was surveyed for them in 1885 by J. C. Nelson, creating a reserve of just seventy-nine square miles.[57] After the death of Long Lodge, his band voted to amalgamate with the Man Who Took the Coat band. In 1891, Man Who Took the Coat died and was succeeded by Carry the Kettle.

CARRY THE KETTLE, *August 1908* (Archives of Manitoba,
Edmund Morris Collection 35, N13610).

CHAPTER EIGHT

The Modern Age

Reserve Life

Treaty 4, signed in 1874, included the Saulteaux, Cree, and Nakoda between Fort Ellice and the Cypress Hills. It resulted from tough negotiations between Alexander Morris, who was then treaty commissioner, and The Gambler and Pasquah, Aboriginal leaders who put at issue the land the Hudson's Bay Company had occupied. Aboriginal nations argued that money for the extinguishment of title from the Company should have gone to the Aboriginal peoples, who had never given up their title, and not to the Canadian government. Eventually, after the government's tactics of separating militant nations from the more passive ones had succeeded, most of the Aboriginal peoples signed the treaty agreements and moved onto reserves.

Many of the Aboriginal people who had congregated in the Cypress Hills settled on reserves at Crooked and Round lakes in the Qu'Appelle Valley during the early 1880s. This was described as "a most beautiful part of the country, right on the Northern edge of the great plains, [with] fine poplar bluffs, some small lakes and the choices of wheat land, an ideal location chosen by the Indians themselves. This had always been a great wintering place for them."[1]

Under the agreement, the Canadian government assumed responsibility to provide seed and materials to treaty nations for farming. In the early years of reserve life (1876-79), however, this was not enough. There was malnutrition — even starvation — on many reserves. The government did not provide an adequate administrative structure; often materials and seed stipulated in the contract were not sent. Many problems arose because a distant government in

Ottawa simply did not understand the people and conditions in the West. In 1876, for example, it was still possible for the minister of the interior, David Mills, to believe that all Aboriginal people were on reserves. Policy decisions that restricted the ability of reserve residents to farm did not further the stated goal of making them self-sufficient agriculturalists. It may well be that solving the problems faced by the Aboriginal people was simply beyond the insights and resources of that generation of whites. These problems were compounded when the starving people who had not initially signed treaties began to turn to the reserves as their hopes for subsistence from game on the plains waned.

Aboriginal policy originated in Ottawa. The earliest policies from the early 1870s were part of a process intended to settle Aboriginal people on reserves. The main task of the first two Boards of Commissions — in 1874 and 1876, respectively — had been to sign treaties with the Aboriginal people, especially in the fertile belt, where settlers were encouraged to take up lands according to the national policy. By 1876, with treaty-making for the most part complete in the Cypress Hills area, changes were made to adapt to the duties that emerged. The Board of Commissions was replaced by a system of Indian superintendents, with two or more Indian agents in each superintendency. Under this arrangement, there were four superintendencies for the area between the Pacific Coast and the Ontario-Manitoba border. In the North-West Superintendency alone, there were 17,000 treaty Indians to administer. The Indian agents had the least amount of time for farm instruction — which was, ironically, what the Aboriginal nations required most.

First Nations interested in learning about mechanized farming practices complained that little teaching was available. In practice, they provided farm instructors with free manual labour without any profit to themselves. Many of the farm instructors hired to assist in developing agricultural skills among the Aboriginal people proved to be inept. Most had little farm experience and were unsuited to dealing with a society different from their own.

The situation proved disastrous. First Nations had been encouraged to settle on reserves, but the agricultural policy the government was proposing was not able to provide them with enough food to survive. Money granted by the treaties proved to be grossly inadequate. There were not even sufficient resources to purchase enough food for basic nutrition. The lack of equipment prevented farming beyond a primitive level. Even when equipment was provided, it usually came without adequate operating instructions. When it was broken, there was no way to repair it. In the end, much of the machinery remained virtually useless.

The instructors had been directed by Ottawa to implement a policy of "work for rations." The Aboriginal people resented this; they thought the rations were a right, not something to be earned. They pointed to the famine clause in Treaty 6, which stipulated that Aboriginal culture demanded sharing with those in need and assistance to the sick. The Cree thought the Canadian government should share with them during times of starvation, just as the Cree had done for them in the past. The "work for rations" policy was intended to instill among them the idea that rations could not be handed out but had to be earned, but First Nations found this paternalism humiliating, and they saw little use in the menial work demanded of them.

No.193 Cree Indians. Maple Creek. N.W.T.

CREE MEN AT MAPLE CREEK. *The Cree used the Hills extensively, often ranging beyond them into Blackfoot territory. At the time of the treaties, the Canadian government feared the consequences of a large concentration of Cree in the Hills, and disallowed reserves in the area. Nekaneet's band refused to leave, and was eventually granted a reserve in the Cypress Hills in 1913, although they did not receive treaty benefits until 1975* (Glenbow Archives, NA-2883-8).

By 1882, John A. Macdonald's government had begun to cut back all programs, and the Home Farm Plan was one of the first casualties. There had been no proper or competent administration, and resources had been woefully inadequate. The problems of farming on reserves were a concern to government officials through the early 1880s, but the only solution they provided was to send more farm instructors and Indian agents. In areas where there were no home farms, little was done to provide instruction beyond sending a farming instructor, if one was available. These were superficial solutions to increasingly complex problems, and Aboriginal nations were beginning to give up on a government that, during the treaty process, had seemed so eager to assist them in adapting to agricultural life on the reserve.[2]

Two home farms had been established in 1879 in the Cypress Hills, one for the Cree and one for the Nakoda. The home farm for the Nakoda was established under John J. English and later became the Horace Greely Ranch. The other home farm was established forty-eight kilometers northeast of Fort Walsh on Maple Creek. Cowesses, or Little Child, had selected a reserve here, and members of his band settled in the area, although the official survey to establish the reserve was never completed. In 1881, Piapot chose a reserve about sixteen kilometers north of the Maple Creek farm.

The Maple Creek farm was supervised by John Setter who, unlike most in the first contingent of farm instructors, was a "man of the country," a son of an HBC man, born at Red River. Agent McDonald reported that Setter had excellent crops after one year, considering that there had been no rain and seeding had been completed late in the season. He noted that the Aboriginal people had displayed a "great deal of energy in trying to make a success of their first agricultural enterprize [sic]."[3] The following year there were 46.5 hectares of wheat, oats, turnips, and potatoes under cultivation at the Maple Creek farm. Some of the Nakoda worked at their farms extremely well. They took pride in their gardens and were annoyed at the unavailability of seed. A number had planted wheat, and, as a result, McDonald recommended that the Maple Creek farm be supplied with a portable grist mill, on the theory that, if the Nakoda could grind their own grain, many more of them could be induced to break land the following year. McDonalod was confident that the Nakoda could be self-sustaining by the next growing season. Despite the fact that the home farm at Maple Creek proved to be one of the great successes of the program, it was closed down in the winter of 1881-82 when the government decided to disallow reserves in the Cypress Hills and move all treaty nations in the area to reserves to the north or east.

Up until 1882, bands of Cree and Nakoda who had not signed Treaties 4 and 6 congregated in the Cypress Hills. Game could still support them, but eventually the large numbers of Aboriginals around Fort Walsh depleted these resources. In 1881, 4,000 Aboriginal people were fed around Fort Walsh. The Aboriginal ranks thinned when Piapot signed Treaty 4 in 1875 and when Little Pine signed Treaty 6 in 1879. Only Big Bear remained in the Cypress Hills, and with him the dream of establishing a large reserve. Big Bear hoped that a large concentration of Cree in the Cypress Hills might force the government into talks that could lead to the fulfillment of treaty promises. The Cree, however, were weakened by starvation, and were unable to maintain a strong position in the Hills. Their forays into the United States in pursuit of the diminishing buffalo herds were less and less successful as the American army was on the lookout to drive the Cree back into Canadian territory.

Big Bear's other hope — to forge an alliance with the Blackfoot and Crow to prevent the destruction of the buffalo herds — was frustrated by the horse stealing that plagued peaceful relations among the tribes. Starving young war-

BIG BEAR'S CAMP NEAR THE CYPRESS HILLS, 1883. *Big Bear came to the Hills with the hope of organizing local First Nations into a united front, but by 1883 starvation had led to conflict among his people, who were in desperate need of government rations, and he resigned himself to moving north onto a reserve* (G. M. Dawson/National Archives of Canada, PA-050746).

riors carried out these raids, and leaders such as Big Bear were powerless to stop them. By late 1882, the same year the NWMP detachment was preparing to move from Fort Walsh to Maple Creek, Big Bear's band was racked with dissension. Many of his followers wanted to sign the treaty in order to receive rations. That year, as the band was camped around Cypress Lake, the decision was made to sign an adhesion to Treaty 6 and move north. Big Bear had no strength left to resist. In the north, he would once again work to unite the Cree in an unsuccessful effort to force the government to deliver on its treaty promises.

The government decision in the winter of 1881-82 to remove First Nations from the Cypress Hills was born out of fear. The usual explanation is that officials feared conflict or collusion among American and Canadian Aboriginal peoples, and they wanted to discourage horse-stealing raids, which they feared might lead to international incidents. A more recent interpretation suggests, however, that Canadian authorities were concerned about the danger posed by a concentration of the Cree on contiguous reserves in the Cypress Hills, as this would effectively create an Aboriginal territory which would be difficult to control.

Thus, Commissioner of Indian Affairs Edgar Dewdney pursued a policy of starving into submission those who had not taken treaty. In 1882-83, the federal government announced new regulations that restricted the payment of annuities to Aboriginal people on reserves only; rationing was discontinued, and Fort Walsh was closed. In pursuing this action, Dewdney violated oral promises he had made in 1880 and 1881 to allow Cree and Nakoda reserves in the Hills. His denial of a reserve in the Cypress Hills to Big Bear was also a violation of written promises made by the Treaty Commissions of both 1874 and 1876.

The Nekaneet Band

There was one band, however, that refused to move. Foremost Man, or Nekaneet, insisted on taking his reserve in the Cypress Hills. After signing Treaty 4, he took his annuity payments at Fort Qu'Appelle, then, in 1879, he began to take payment at Fort Walsh. Even after others in his band had settled in the Qu'Appelle area, Nekaneet remained on the plains around the Cypress Hills with other independent Cree. In 1881, he and his band ranged as far south as the Missouri River before American authorities intercepted, disarmed, and escorted them back to Canada.

After the winter of 1882-83, when the new government regulations about annuity payments were introduced and rationing was discontinued, many Indians left Nekaneet's band to settle on reserves away from the Hills. These actions did not discourage the most committed of Nekaneet's band, however, even though the number of members declined from 428 in 1881 to 350 in 1883, and to 119 in 1898. Even when Fort Walsh was abandoned in 1883, and the NWMP detachment moved to Maple Creek, the Cree continued to stay in the Cypress Hills.

In these years Nekaneet continued to press his claims for a reserve in the Hills:

> I have been born and have lived in this part of the country where I was raised in. I have always been a loyal subject to Her Majesty's Government and whenever I meet white People I have always been friendly to them. I showed my loyalty when there was trouble in 1885 by keeping my Band quiet.[4]

Through the 1890s, the Canadian government continually attempted to induce the Aboriginal people to settle on reserves. Many tactics were used. Hayter Reed, eventually deputy superintendent of Indian Affairs, tried to label Foremost Man's band as troublemakers, even though there was little evidence of this and their relations with the local white community were good. The people in his band never asked for government assistance. One police officer observed:

> If we do not happen to find out their condition they will say nothing as they are morbidly afraid of accepting assistance from the government least they should be compelled to go and live on a reserve. One is disposed to think that life on any kind of reserve must be better than the life they lead, but they cannot be persuaded to think so.[5]

Nekaneet died in 1897 before his dream of a reserve in the Cypress Hills was realized. The Canadian government finally relented and granted the descendants of Nekaneet's band a reserve in 1913, giving it his name. It was not until 1975 that the government agreed to pay the band its treaty benefits, after they had lived without them for ninety-three years.

CREE WOMAN AT FORT WALSH. *Women played a crucial role in helping the Cree survive as their people experienced severe times of want as the buffalo disappeared. They were especially resourceful in gathering berries and snaring small game as their people moved onto reserves* (Glenbow Archives, NA-2446-9).

Aboriginal Women on the Reserve

Starvation was constantly on the horizon for Aboriginal people as their lifestyles changed, and women became an essential economic component of reserve life by learning new skills and adapting old ones. Their adaptability helped diversify the food supply and contributed to risk-reduction for fragile reserve economies. The hard work of women was not their only contribution. They were also a spiritual inspiration to their communities. As one Cree observer noted, "Theirs was the satisfaction of making their loved ones happy. Their cheerfulness could not help but be infectious, thus everyone was soon striving to do his share and the Crees were able to look on the bright side of things."[6]

Restricted movement meant that foraging activities were not conducted over as large an area as they had once been. Nevertheless, wild fruits remained a staple, and included saskatoons, raspberries and strawberries, black currants, and choke cherries. Wild rhubarb was used in soups, and kinnikinnik was gathered as a tobacco substitute. Sap from birch and maple trees was boiled and manufactured into syrup. Roots such as wild turnip were collected and dried. Seneca root was collected for trade, as well as for home use as a medicine. Fish were caught and smoked by women throughout the spring and summer. Wild fowl were caught, plucked, and dried, as were other small game such as rabbit, prairie chicken, and gopher. Much of the work of collecting, hunting, and food preparation was done communally, and the activities and excursions were characterized by a spirit of high morale and humour.

Hauling water and wood were the daily heavy work done by women to maintain their households. Offsetting this hard work was the weaving — more commonly done in winter — when hats and baskets were made of rushes and willows that had been collected in the warmer months. Clothes were made and repaired throughout the year, but more commonly in the winter. Other, more labour-intensive work was grinding grain into flour and the continual tanning of hides.

Many of these activities changed little from pre-reserve days, but there were new forms of labour undertaken by women during the reserve era. Many of these were associated with agriculture. Working in grain fields, stooking, gathering, and binding sheaves were all new skills the women had to learn. Other skills adapted for the reserve era that required women's labour included making butter and bread, milking, knitting, mending, soap making, gardening, caring for poultry, and calving. As well, women were often called upon to make repairs to huts or cabins that had been built from poor lumber that often provided only the barest of shelter. Reserve poverty left most families with minimal housing:

> . . . low, one-storey, one-room log structures with mud roofs and wood fireplaces. Many had flooring by the late 1880s, but few had amenities such as glass windows, banks or bedsteads, cooking stoves, chairs, dishes, and coal lamps. The open fireplace, made of upright posts covered with a thick coating of clay mixed with water, provided both heat and light. The chimney, always open, served as ventilator. The sleeping places were seldom more than a bundle of rags on the floor.[7]

The conditions that women had to cope with in their homes were as bad as the poor anywhere had to contend with. But they managed to survive, as many have noted, with resiliency and often with humour.

The Ranching Era

The cattle industry in the Cypress Hills began with the NWMP herds that were brought in to feed starving Aboriginal people between 1879 and 1883. The cattle were brought to Fort Walsh from the south through contracts for beef with the I. G. Baker Co. Before the disappearance of the buffalo, there had been no cattle to speak of, because on the open range domestic bulls were killed by the buffalo bulls and their cows would drift off with the buffalo herds.

The first cattle ranchers in the Cypress Hills settled near the fort in the years before the CPR passed through Maple Creek in 1883. The first ranchers close to the site of Fort Walsh were Wellington Anderson and David Wood. They brought their cattle out from Manitoba in the early 1890s on a drive that took them two months. The pair remained partners for twenty-five years. A number of other ranches, including those of the Lawrences and Pollocks, were established in the 1880s and 1890s. John Linder, born in Germany, brought twenty head of cattle and ten horses to the Fort Walsh area. He and his four sons occupied an enormous expanse of leased land extending over seventy-two sections. Everett Parsonage from England homesteaded just south of Battle Creek, and James Gaff came from Kansas and Nebraska before settling next to the Linder place. Eventually ranch homes were dotted along all the creeks flowing north and south from the Cypress Hills: Fish Creek, Piapot Creek, Bear Creek, Battle Creek, and Skull Creek.

The settlers were from a wide variety of backgrounds and included a number of Métis families. John Laframboise and his family established themselves at Piapot Creek in the mid-1880s. Jules Quesnell, who had herded cattle for the I. G. Baker Co., worked for a time on the Oxarart Ranch and settled at Hay Creek, as did Celistine St. Denis. Francis Xavier Swain, who was married to Mary Breland (great-granddaughter of the Métis leader Cuthbert Grant),[8] settled in the Skull Creek district. A native person from Manitoba, John Tanner, who once ran mail for the NWMP, also tried to establish a farm in the Hills, but as a treaty Indian he was not allowed to homestead.

There were a number of famous large ranches in the area, including the Oxarart Ranch, which was established in the early 1880s near Battle Creek. The owners were Basques from the Pyrenees who brought 300 head of horses and took out leases for a 4,048-hectare grazing area. They imported thoroughbred horses from England and the United States, and owned the famous race horse Blair Athol, who was ridden by John Léveillé. The Léveillé brothers were the cowboys on this ranch, which grew to have a herd of 1,700 that at one time grazed an area that was said to have run from the Cypress Hills to the Milk River and the Alberta border to Val Marie. Other large ranches at the turn of the twentieth century were those of the Pollock Brothers, the Cheeseman Brothers, the Dixon Brothers, and Horace Greely. It was not until 1906 that farmers were attracted to the area and began to change the way of life. The property on which Fort Walsh stands was sold to the RCMP by Frank Nuttall in 1942. The Mounties reconstructed a number of buildings from 1943 to 1967; many of the structures reconstructed were based on those in the original fort.

Fort Walsh National Historic Site

Fort Walsh was dismantled and abandoned in 1883. By the 1890s, the site had become the headquarters for the Wood and Anderson ranching operation. Ranching activity continued on the site until the early 1940s, when the RCMP acquired the property and constructed a remount ranch on the site of the original fort to breed horses for the force's equestrian training and the famous Musical Ride. When the RCMP remount operation was moved to Ontario in 1968, the property was transferred to the Canadian Parks Service.

In 1972, Fort Walsh was formally declared a national historic site, encompassing a land base of 650 hectares, which makes it one of the larger sites in the national system of historic parks and sites. Despite this relatively recent designation as a national historic site, Fort Walsh had been declared a site of national historic significance by the Historic Sites and Monuments Board of Canada in 1924. This was followed in 1926 by the erection of a commemorative plaque and cairn to recognize Fort Walsh as a centre of law and order in the Canadian West. In 1964, the Historic Sites and Monuments Board further recommended that the Cypress Hills Massacre be recognized as an event of national significance "because of its influence on the passage of the bill to establish the North-West Mounted Police."[9] During Canada's Centennial in 1967, the board reinforced the significance of Fort Walsh by recommending that its founder and commander, James Morrow Walsh, be commemorated as an "eminent Canadian."

Since 1968, the Canadian Parks Service has developed a visitor program and maintenance operation at Fort Walsh National Historic Site that is centred on the reconstructed buildings of the fort and Farwell's and Solomon's trading posts. In 1976, the Canadian Parks Service opened a visitor reception centre with an exhibit hall, audio-visual theatre, food services, an internal transportation system, and a seasonal staff of interpreters who present the Fort Walsh story through tours and special programs. The operation of the park, which is open to the public from mid-May to Thanksgiving, is supported by a small administrative staff based in Maple Creek, Saskatchewan.

Each National Historic Site represents some aspect of Canadian history. Their theme statements provide the historic rationale and national context for the planning and development of an historic site so that its resources are conserved, commemorated, managed, and interpreted in an appropriate manner. Three primary themes — Native People in the Cypress Hills; Whoop-Up Country and the Cypress Hills Massacre; The NWMP and Canadian Sovereignty in the Northwest — and one secondary theme — Ranching and the Remount Station Era — have been identified to present the story of the fort in the Cypress Hills in a comprehensive historic context.[10] Since 2000, Fort Walsh National Historic Site has been part of the agreement that created Cypress Hills Interprovincial Park in 1989, Canada's first and only interprovincial park.[11]

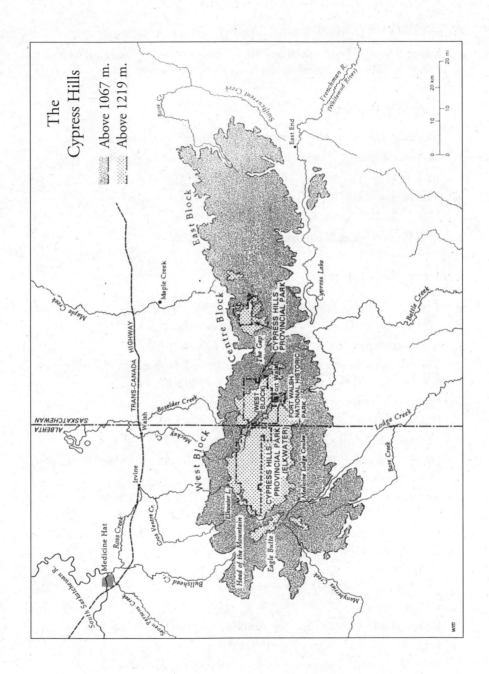

The
Cypress Hills

Above 1067 m.
Above 1219 m.

East Block

Centre Block

West Block

Maple Creek

TRANS-CANADA HIGHWAY

SASKATCHEWAN
ALBERTA

Walsh

Irvine

Medicine Hat

The Gap

CYPRESS HILLS
PROVINCIAL PARK

Fort Walsh

FORT WALSH
NATIONAL HISTORIC
PARK

(WEST
BLOCK)

CYPRESS HILLS
PROVINCIAL PARK
(ELKWATER)

Elkwater L.

Head of the Mountain

Eagle Butte

Medicine Lodge Coulee

Battle Creek

Cypress Lake

Lodge Creek

Bare Creek

East End

Frenchman R.
(Whitemud River)

Swiftcurrent Creek

Battle Creek

Boxelder Creek

Mackay Cr.

Maple Creek

Ross Creek

Gros Ventre Cr.

Bullshead Cr.

Manyberries Creek

Seven Persons Creek

South Saskatchewan R.

20 km
0   10   20
0   10   20 mi

wm

NOTES

NOTES TO CHAPTER ONE

1 Candace Savage, "Eight Thousand Years Down," pp. 80-88; and Ann Chandler, "Digging History — Secrets of the Great Plains," pp. 30-32.

NOTES TO CHAPTER TWO

1 Alexander Henry the Elder, *Travels and Adventures in Canada*, pp. 299-300.

2 Glyndwr Williams, "The Hudson's Bay Company and the Fur Trade," p. 35.

3 *Ibid.*, p. 42.

4 John Milloy, *The Plains Cree*, p. 186.

5 Eleanor Burke Leacock, "Montagnais Women."

6 Alan Michael Klein, "Adaptive Strategies on the Plains."

NOTES TO CHAPTER THREE

1 E. E. Rich, *The Fur Trade*, p. 240.

2 John E. Sunder, *The Fur Trade on the Upper Missouri*, p. 258.

3 T. Lindsay Baker, "Beaver to Buffalo Robes," no. 2, p. 6.

4 Margaret Anne Kennedy and Brian O. K. Reeves, *An Inventory of Whiskey Posts*, Vol. I, pp. 27-28; Paul F. Sharp, *Whoop-Up Country*, pp. 44-45.

5 Georgia G. Fooks, "Fort Whoop-Up," p. 6.

6 Paul F. Sharp, *Whoop-Up Country*, pp. 48-49.

7 Abel Farwell, *Inventory Ledgers*.

8 Henry C. Klassen, "International Enterprise," p. 58; and James M. Francis, "Montana Business," p. 292.

9 Rhoda R. Gilman, "The Upper Mississippi Fur Trade," p. 123. Gilman noted the number and value of furs sold in the US actually increased from 1830 to 1870.

10 Baker, "Beaver to Buffalo Robes," no. 2, p. 6; Georgia G. Fooks, "Fort Whoop-Up," p. 23; and "Paid to Hammond, June 6, 1872," T. C. Power Papers, Box 277, Folder 8.

11 Baker, "Beaver to Buffalo Robes," no. 2, p. 6.

12 *Ibid.*, p. 11.

13 Robson Bonnichsen and Stuart J. Baldwin, "Cypress Hills," App. 3, p. 77.

14 Jacqueline Peterson, "Many Roads to Red River," pp. 38-39.

15 Andy Den Otter, "Transportation, Trade and Regional Identity," p. 4.

16 Clovis Rondeau, *La Montagne de Bois*, pp. 10-11.

17 *Ibid.*, p. 11.

18 *Ibid.*, p. 15.

19 Isaac Cowie, *The Company of Adventurers,* pp. 431, 462. Cowie believed the establishment of his post led other traders and Indians to violate what he thought was the traditional neutrality of the Hills to exploit its animal resources.

20 *Ibid.*, pp. 432-37.

21 Sharp, *Whoop-Up Country,* p. 39.

22 Gerald L. Berry, *The Whoop-Up Trail,* pp. 39-41; Kennedy and Reeves, *An Inventory of Whiskey Posts,* Vol. I, pp. 13-14; and Fooks, "Fort Whoop-Up," p. 38.

23 Paul C. Phillips, "The Fur Trade in Montana," p. 60.

24 Sharp, *Merchant Princes,* pp. 7-9.

25 James M. Francis, "Montana Business," p. 296.

26 *Ibid.*, pp. 292-93.

27 Henry C. Klassen, "I. G. Baker," p. 42.

28 Klassen, "International Enterprise," p. 292.

29 Peter Darby, "River Boats to Rail Lines," p. 13.

30 Dr. John E. Foster, personal communication, Jan. 8, 1992.

31 Kennedy and Reeves, *An Inventory of Whiskey Posts,* Vol. I, p. 15.

32 Darby, "River Boats to Rail Lines," p. 13.

33 Margaret Anne Kennedy, "A Whiskey Trade Frontier," pp. 59-60.

34 Francis Paul Prucha, *Indian Policy,* p. 72.

35 Sharp, *Merchant Princes,* p. 5; and Henry C. Klassen, "I. G. Baker," p. 43.

36 Mary L. Weeks, *The Last Buffalo Hunter,* p. 153.

37 Sharp, *Whoop-Up Country,* p. 42; Kennedy and Reeves, *An Inventory of Whiskey Posts,* Vol. I, p. 14; and Fooks, "Fort Whoop-Up," p. 2.

38 Brian Hubner, "'The Farwellians.'"

39 Hugh A. Dempsey, "Sweet Grass Hills Massacre," p. 13; and Henry C. Klassen, "International Enterprise," p. 42.

40 Lewis O. Saum, "From Vermont to Whoop-Up Country," p. 57; and Dan L. Tharpp, *Encyclopedia of Frontier Biography,* "J. J. Healy," Vol. II, p. 637.

41 Sharp, *Merchant Princes,* p. 5. Sharp claimed the trade was built "out of ruins" of the American Fur Company.

42 Kennedy and Reeves, *An Inventory of Whiskey Posts,* Vol. II, p. 171; Tharpp, *Encyclopedia of Frontier Biography,* "Joe Kipp," Vol. II, pp. 787-88; D. B. Sealy, "Jerry Potts," *Dictionary of Canadian Biography,* Vol. 12, pp. 858-59.

43 Kennedy, "A Whiskey Trade Frontier," p. 65.

44 W. Henry McKay, "The Story of Edward McKay," pp. 76-77, 100-01, 105.

45   Kennedy, "A Whiskey Trade Frontier," p. 310.

46   Kennedy and Reeves, *An Inventory of Whiskey Posts,* Vol. I, p. ii; Jack Elliott, "Tradition and Fact," p. 19; and Philip Goldring, "Whiskey, Horses and Death," p. 47. Goldring stated that there were thirteen traders in 1873 in the Cypress Hills, operating within a 4.8-kilometre radius.

47   A. B. McCullough, Papers, pp. 9-10.

NOTES TO CHAPTER FOUR

1   This is based on the 1870 US census, which included a 28-year-old Abel Farwell, born in Massachusetts, living in Dawson County, and a 36-year-old A. C. Farwell, born in New York and living in Fort Benton. These two Farwells may refer to the same person, as the Dawson County census was taken at a later date.

2   George Lande, taped interview, April 10, 1991; and the *Winnipeg Standard,* June 24, 1876.

3   Anon., "Old Fort Peck," p. 2.

4   Abel Farwell Inventory Ledgers for 1869, 1870, 1871, pp. 72-74; and 1872 "Petty Ledger 'D'"; Abel Farwell, "Cypress Mountains"; and Isaac Cowie, *The Company of Adventurers,* p. 388.

5   Margaret Anne Kennedy, personal communication, Dec. 7, 1989; and Margaret Anne Kennedy and Brian O. K. Reeves, *An Inventory of Whiskey Posts,* Vol. I, p. 73.

6   Margaret Anne Kennedy, "A Whiskey Trade Frontier," pp. 251-52.

7   Hugh A. Dempsey, "Sweet Grass Hills Massacre," pp. 14-15.

8   Jack Elliott, "Tradition and Fact," pp. 8-9, 15-17.

9   The *Helena Daily Independent,* "The Extradition Trial," July 15, 1875; and George Lande, taped interview, April 10, 1991.

10   Bureau of Indian Affairs, file 30 SA.

11   Hammond/Coombes/Beckwith, "Family Genealogy."

12   L. J. Hammond, "Certificate of Membership."

13   Joel Overholser, personal communication, Dec. 14, 1989.

14   Bob Saindon and Bunky Sullivan, "Taming the Missouri," p. 36.

15   Anon., *Progressive Men of Montana,* p. 1678.

16   Georgia G. Fooks, "Fort Whoop-Up," pp. 7-8.

17   Charles Rowe, "The Bluff of Fred Kanouse."

18   T. C. Power Papers, June 6, 1872.

19   Dan Kennedy, *Recollection of an Assiniboine Chief,* p. 42.

20   Philip Goldring, *Whisky, Horses and Death,* p. 47; and the *Winnipeg Standard,* June 24, 1876.

21 Anon., *Progressive Men of Montana,* p. 1678; and 1900 US Census.

22 Hazel Jacobsen, *Profile of Early Ovando,* pp. 49-50.

23 T. R. McCloy, "The descendants"; and personal communication, July 10, 1990.

24 Jacqueline Peterson. "Many roads to Red River: Métis genesis in the Great Lakes Region," in *The New Peoples: Being and Becoming Metis in North America,* pp. 38-39.

25 *Winnipeg Standard,* "Trial of the Cypress Hills Murderers," June 24, 1876.

26 Dale L. Morgan and Eleanor Towles Harris (Eds.), "The biography of Etienne Provost," pp. 345-46. Alexis may have also worked for the HBC in this period, as related by J. J. Healy in "Bucking the Hudson's Bay Company, pp. 15-17; and Annie Heloise Abel (Ed.), *Chardon's Journal at Fort Clark, 1834-1839,* pp. 38, 44, 301, note 378.

27 D. N. Sprague and R. R. Fry (Comps.), *The Genealogy of the First Métis Nation: The Development and Dispersal of the Red River Settlement,* Tables 1 and 3; and Sherry Farrell Racette, "Sewing ourselves together: Clothing, decorative arts and the expression of Métis and half breed identity," pp. 235-36.

28 Charles Larpenteur. *Forty Years a Fur Trader,* Vol. I, pp. 80, 87-91.

29 St. John's Baptisms. E.4/1a; fo. 126, Archives of Manitoba (currently in the Anglican Church Archives).

30 John James Audubon, *Audubon and His Journals,* Vol. I, p. 529, and Vol. II, pp. 9, 16 & 39.

31 Racette, "Sewing ourselves together," pp. 238-39.

32 Rudolph Friederich Kurz. *Journal of Rudolph Friederich Kurz,* p. 224 (photo), pp. 254, 324.

33 Jack Holtman. *King of the High Missouri. The saga of the Culbertsons,* pp. 94-95.

34 Anon., *Contributions to the Historical Society of Montana,* Vol. 10, 1940: *The Fort Benton and Fort Sarpy Journal, 1855-1856,* p. 295, note 322. For Labombarde at Fort Sarpy, see pp. 151-53, 157.

35 Isaac Ingalls Stevens. *Report of Exploration of a Route for the Pacific Railroad, near the Forty-seventh and Forty-ninth Parallels, from St. Paul to Puget Sound,* pp. 351-55.

36 Canadian Sessional Papers, Vol. 13, p. 384; as quoted in Lawrence Barkwell, "Labombarde, Alexis," *Batoche 1885: The Militia of the Métis Liberation Movement,* p. 22.

37 Goldring, *Whisky, Horses and Death,* p. 47; *Winnipeg Standard,* June 24, 1879; and Overholser, personal communication, June 25, 1991.

38 This is the description of Solomon by his granddaughter, who knew him. Winniefred Eastlund Arhelger, "Moses Salomon," p. 2.

39 The name was usually written Solomon or Soloman, although he was born Salomon, and the first name was rendered as Moses or Mose.

40 Arhelger, p. 1.

41 Joel Overholser, *Fort Benton*, pp. 145-47; and *The Kendall Miner*, "Tribute to His Memory," Aug. 31, 1906, in Arhelger, p. 4.

42 Moses Solomon was first mentioned at Fort Benton in 1865. Overholser, personal communication, Nov. 3, 1989.

43 Jim Wood, personal communication, Aug. 9, 1922. Solomon travelled to Fort Peck in 1866 in a mackinaw and he appears on a Deer Lodge passenger list.

44 T. C. Power Papers, Petty Ledger "A" 1867-70, "H" 1869-70, "D" 1872-74, "B" 1870-72, #2 1869, "C" 1871-72. Solomon purchased supplies from T. C. Power in the period 1867-74.

45 Kennedy and Reeves, *An Inventory of Whiskey Posts*, Vol. I, p. 124.

46 Jack Elliott, "Tradition and Fact," pp. 7-8, 17, 19, 40.

47 Goldring, *Whisky, Horses and Death*, p. 47.

48 Dempsey, "Sweet Grass Hills Massacre," pp. 12-18; and Joel Overholser, personal communication, Nov. 3, 1989.

49 Goldring, p. 51.

50 *Ibid.*, p. 53.

51 *Ibid.*

52 *Ibid.*

53 *Winnipeg Standard*, June 24, 1876.

54 John Peter Turner, *The North-West Mounted Police, 1873-1893*, Vol. I, p. 219.

55 Samuel B. Steele. *Forty Years in Canada*, p. 36.

56 Goldring, p. 56.

NOTES TO CHAPTER FIVE

1 Edwin Charles Morgan, *North-West Mounted Police*, pp. 92-93.

2 A. Wilson, *The Letters of Charles John Brydges*, p. 47.

3 *Ibid.*, p. 37.

4 *Ibid.*, p. 157. Smith and Kavanaugh were competing tenderers for government contracts.

5 T. C. Powers Papers, 55-106-9, Jan. 27, 1880.

6 Wallace E. Stegner, *Wolf Willow*, p. 303.

7 John Peter Turner, *The North-West Mounted Police*, Vol. I, p. 496.

1   John Milloy, *The Plains Cree*; Arthur Ray, *Indians in the Fur Trade*.

2   Milloy, *The Plains Cree*, pp. 266-67.

3   Frederick Turner, *Beyond Geography*.

4   Irene Spry, "The Transition from a Nomadic to a Settled Economy in Western Canada, 1856-96," p. 204.

5   *Ibid.*, p. 205.

6   *Ibid.*, p. 211.

7   Gerald Friesen, *The Canadian Prairies*, p. 20.

8   Sarah Carter, *Lost Harvests*, p. 54.

9   *Ibid.*, p. 55.

10 *Ibid.*

11 *Ibid.*, p. 56.

12 *Ibid.*, p. 57.

13 *Ibid.*, p. 58.

14 Robert Utley, *The Lance and the Shield*, pp. 14-15, 22.

15 John Peter Turner, *The North-West Mounted Police*, Vol. I, p. 290.

16 John S. Gray, *Custer's Last Campaign*, pp. 373-400.

17 Ellen McLeod, *Fort Walsh*, pp. 39-44.

18 Turner, *The North-West Mounted Police*, Vol. I, p. 364.

19 *Ibid.*, p. 468.

20 Grant MacEwan, "Sitting Bull"; entry in the *Dictionary of Canadian Biography*, Vol. 11, p. 870.

21 Turner, *The North-West Mounted Police*, Vol. I, p. 587.

22 MacEwan, "Sitting Bull."

23 *Ibid.*

24 William A. Waiser, "The North-West Mounted Police."

25 Parliament of Canada, *House of Commons Sessional Papers*, No. 116, A. 1885, pp. 31-36.

26 McKenzie, N. M. W. J. "The Men of the Hudson's Bay Company," pp. 70-71.

27 Anon., *Epitome of Parliamentary Documents in Connection with the North-West Rebellion, 1885*, pp. 298-304.

28 Adrian Gabriel Morice, *Dictionaire historique des Canadiens et des Metis francais de l' Ouest*, p. 138.

29 Department of the Interior, North-West Scrip Commission, 1885, Vol. 1475. "Alexis Labombarbe," [sic] p. 50, no. 1155, claim no 1635; "Nancy Kipling," p. 41, no. 977, claim no. 1636.

NOTES TO CHAPTER SEVEN

1   United States Court of Federal Claims, *The Assiniboine Indian Tribe* v. *The United States*, 1929.

2   Edwin Thompson Denig, *Five Indian Tribes of the Upper Missouri*, pp. 63-98.

3   Denig, *Five Indian Tribes*; see also George Catlin, *Letters and Notes on the Manners. Customs and Conditions of North American Indians*. For alliances the Nakoda entered into, see elders' testimony in *Assiniboine* v. *United States*, 1929.

4   Carry the Kettle Archives, interviews with elders. Chief Talks Different suggested that the Nakoda, when gathered, had 7,700 lodges with ten to twelve people per lodge.

5   Dan Kennedy, *Recollections of an Assiniboine Chief.*

6   *Assiniboine* v. *United States.*

7   Carry the Kettle Archives.

8   *The Treaties of Canada with the Indians*, pp. 77–125.

9   Carry the Kettle Archives.

10 *Ibid.*

11 McIllree to Dewdney Feb. 15, 1882.

12 Adhesion to Treaty 4, signed by Chiefs Man Who Took the Coat and Long Lodge, Sept. 25, 1877.

13 Patrick to Dewdney, Dec. 16, 1880.

14 Sarah Carter, *Lost Harvest.*

15 Superintendent General of Indian Affairs (S.G.I.A.) to Governor General, Dec. 31, 1881.

16 *Ibid.*

17 Quoted in *Our Pioneers*, South Western Saskatchewan Oldtimers Association, pp. 39-40.

18 Dewdney to S.G.I.A., Jan 1, 1882.

19 Wadsworth to Vankoughnet, Aug. 29, 1881.

20 Dewdney to S.G.I.A.

21 Carter, *Lost Harvest*, p. 112.

22 *Ibid.*

23 John Tobias, "Canada's Subjugation of the Plains Cree, 1879-1885," pp. 519–48.

24 S.G.I.A. to Governor General, Dec. 31, 1881.

25 Wadsworth to Dewdney, July 3, 1880.

26 Vankoughnet to Macdonald, Oct. 10, 1881.

27 Denny to Dewdney, Jan. 9, 1882.

28 McIllree to Dewdney, Feb. 15, 1882.

29 Carry the Kettle Archives.

30 Galt to Dewdney, July 18, 1881.

31 Wadsworth to Vankoughnet, Aug. 29, 1881.

32 Allen to Galt, June 27, 1881.

33 Denny to Dewdney, Nov. 20, 1881.

34 Denny to Dewdney, Nov. 9, 1881.

35 Galt to Macdonald, May 24, 1881.

36 Irvine to White, May 30, 1882.

37 Carry the Kettle Archives.

38 Department of Indian Affairs to Dewdney, May 11, 1882.

39 Galt to McDonald, June 20, 1882.

40 McDonald to Galt, July 29, 1882.

41 McDonald to Galt, July 31, 1882.

42 *Ibid.*

43 McDonald to Galt, Aug. 1, 1882.

44 Hourie to McDonald, Oct. 18, 1882.

45 Dewdney to Irvine, Oct. 27, 1882.

46 Jukes Report, Oct. 17, 1882.

47 Dewdney to Irvine, Oct. 27, 1882.

48 McIllree to Dewdney, Dec. 2, 1882.

49 Norman to Dewdney, Dec. 27, 1882.

50 I. G. Baker Co. to Galt, Feb. 14, 1882.

51 Dewdney to McDonald, May 25, 1883.

52 Carry the Kettle Archives.

53 Edwards to McDonald, May 13, 1884.

54 Edwards to McDonald, May 13, 1884.

55 Edwards to McDonald, May 20, 1884.

56 Nelson to S.G.I.A., Dec 29, 1882.

57 Nelson to Dewdney, Dec. 5, 1885.

NOTES TO CHAPTER EIGHT

1   John Peter Turner, *The North-West Mounted Police*, pp. 508-59.

2   Sarah Carter, *Lost Harvests,* chap. 2.

3   *Ibid.,* p. 179.

4   David Lee, "Foremost Man and His Band," p. 97. Nekaneet's band did not join the Cree in the 1885 Rebellion.

5   *Ibid.,* p. 112.

6   Carter, *Lost Harvests,* p. 177.

7   *Ibid.,* p. 179.

8   Cuthbert Grant led the Métis against the governor of Red River, Robert Semple, at the Battle of Seven Oakes in 1816.

9   Although the bill creating the NWMP was in place at the time of the massacre, it had not yet been enacted.

10   Anon., "Fort Walsh Management Plan."

11   Cypress Hills Interprovincial Park, www.cypresshills.com/.

BIBLIOGRAPHY

Abel, Annie Heloise, ed. *Chardon's Journal at Fort Clarke 1834-1839*. Pierre: Department of History, State of South Dakota, 1932.

Anon. "Old Fort Peck." *Fort Peck, A Job Well Done, Oct. 1933-Aug. 1977*. Fort Peck Reunion Committee. Glasgow: Ne Mont Printer, 1977.

_____. "Fort Walsh Management Plan." Winnipeg: Canadian Parks Service, 1992.

_____. "The Fort Benton and Fort Sarpy Journal, 1855-1856." *Contributions to the Historical Society of Montana*, Vol. 10, 1940. Helena: Naegele Printing Co., 1940.

_____. *Epitome of Parliamentary Documents in Connection with the North-West Rebellion, 1885*. Ottawa: Maclean, Roger & Co., 1886.

_____. *Progressive Men of Montana*. Chicago: A. W. Bowen & Co., 1903.

Arhelger, Winniefred Eastlund. "Moses Salomon," ms., 1990. Fort Walsh National Historic Site library, Maple Creek, Saskatchewan.

Audubon, John James. *Audubon and His Journals*, Vol. I, p. 529, ed. Maria R. Audubon. New York: Dover Publishing, 1960; and Vol. II, ed. Maria R. Audubon. Glouster, Mass.: Peter Smith Publishing, 1972.

Baker, T. Lindsay. "Beaver to Buffalo Robes: Transition in the Fur Trade." *The Museum of the Fur Trade Quarterly* 23, nos. 1 & 2 (Spring and Summer 1987): 1-8, 4-13.

Barkwell, Lawrence. "Labombarde, Alexis," *Batoche 1885: The Militia of the Métis Liberation Movement*. Canadian Sessional Papers, Vol. 13, p. 38. Winnipeg: Manitoba Métis Federation, 2005.

Berry, Gerald L. *The Whoop-Up Trail: Early Days in Alberta-Montana*. Edmonton: Applied Art Products Ltd., 1953.

Bonnichsen, Robson and Stuart J. Baldwin, "Cypress Hills Ethnohistory and Ecology," *Archaeological Survey of Alberta*, Occasional Paper No. 10. Edmonton: Alberta Culture and Historical Resources, 1978.

Bureau of Indian Affairs files. Crow Agency, Montana.

Cardiff, Daryl. "The Diplomatic Imbroglio Over the Sioux in Canada and the Terry Commission of 1877," ms., 1990. Lethbridge, Alberta: University of Lethbridge.

Carry the Kettle Archives, interviews with elders.

Carter, Sarah. *Lost Harvests: Prairie Reserve Farmers and Government Policy*. Montreal: McGill-Queen's University Press, 1990.

Catlin, George. *Letters and Notes on the Manners, Customs and Conditions of North American Indians*. New York: Dover, 1973.

Chandler, Ann. "Digging History — Secrets of the Great Plains." *The Beaver*, (Vol. 86:3) June/July 2006.

The Commissioners of the Royal North-West Mounted Police. *Opening Up The West, 1874-1881; Being The Official Reports To Parliament Of The Activities Of The Royal North-West Mounted Police Force, from 1874-1881.* Toronto: Coles Publishing Co., Toronto, 1973.

_____. *Settlers and Rebels, 1882-1885; Being The Official Reports To Parliament Of The Activities Of The Royal North-West Mounted Police Force, from 1874-1881.* Toronto: Coles Publishing Co., 1973.

Cowie, Isaac. *The Company of Adventurers: A Narrative of Seven Years in the Service of the Hudson's Bay Company During 1867-1874 on the Great Buffalo Plains.* Toronto: William Briggs, 1913.

Cypress Hills Interprovincial Park, www.cypresshills.com/.

Darby, Peter. "From River Boats to Rail Lines: Circulation Patterns in the Canadian West during the Last Quarter of the Nineteenth Century." *Essays in the Historical Geography of the Canadian West: Regional Perspectives of the Settlement Process,* pp. 5-26. Edited by L. A. Rosenvall and S. M. Evans. Calgary: University of Calgary, Geography Dept., 1987.

Dempsey, Hugh A. "Cypress Hills Massacre." *Montana: The Magazine of Western History,* 3, no. 4 (Autumn 1953): 1-9.

_____. "Sweet Grass Hills Massacre." *Montana: The Magazine of Western History* 7, no. 2 (April 1957): 12-18.

Den Otter, Andy. "Transportation, Trade and Regional Identity in the Southwestern Prairies." *Prairie Forum* 15, no. 1 (Spring 1990): 1-23.

Denig, Edwin Thompson. *Five Indian Tribes of the Upper Missouri: Sioux, Arickara, Assiniboine, Crees and Crow.* Norman: University of Oklahoma Press, 1968, 1973.

Department of the Interior, North-West Scrip Commission, 1885, Alphabetical list, known as Book E. Reel No. 11872, Vol. 1475. "Alexis Labombarbe," [sic] p. 50, no. 1155, claim no 1635; "Nancy Kipling," p. 41, no. 977, claim no. 1636.

Elliott, Jack. "Tradition and Fact — Archaeological Examination of the Cypress Hills Massacre." National Historic Service Report No. 86. Ottawa: Manuscript NHSS Series, 1972.

Ewers, John C. *The Blackfeet: Raiders of the Northwest Plains.* Norman: University of Oklahoma, 1958.

Farwell, Abel. Inventory Ledgers for 1869, 1870, 1871, and 1872. "Life in Whoop-Up Country" file. Fort Walsh National Historic Site Library, Maple Creek, Saskatchewan.

Fooks, Georgia G. "Fort Whoop-Up — Alberta's First and Most Notorious Whiskey Fort." Whoop-Up Country Chapter, Historical Society of Alberta Occasional Paper No. 11. Lethbridge: Historical Society of Alberta, 1983.

Foster, John E. Personal communication, Jan. 8, 1992. Edmonton, Alberta.

Francis, James M. "Montana Business and Canadian Regionalism in the 1870s and 1880s." *The Western Historical Quarterly* 12 (July 1981): 291-304.

Friesen, Gerald. *The Canadian Prairies: A History.* Toronto: University of Toronto Press, 1984.

Gilman, Rhoda R. "Last Days of the Upper Mississippi Fur Trade." *Minnesota History* 42 (1970): 122-40.

Goldring, Philip. *Whisky, Horses and Death: The Cypress Hills Massacre and its Sequel.* Occasional Papers in Archaeology and History, No. 21. Ottawa: National Historic Service, 1973.

Gray, John S. *Custer's Last Campaign: Mitch Boyer and the Little Bighorn Reconstructed.* Lincoln: University of Nebraska Press, 1991.

Hammond, L. J. Personal communication, April 15, 1991. Deer Lodge, Montana.

_____. "Certificate of Membership — Sons and Daughters of Montana Pioneers," Deer Lodge, Montana.

Hammond, Coombes and Beckwith, "Family Genealogy." Courtesy of L. J. Hammond, Deer Lodge, Montana.

Healy, John J. "Bucking the Hudson Bay Company. Told by Captain John J. Healy. Written by Forrest Crissey." *Saturday Evening Post*, pp. 15-17, June 20, 1903.

Henry, Alexander, the Elder. *Travels and Adventures in Canada and the Indian Territories Between the Years 1760-1776.* Edited by James Bain. Toronto: George N. Morany, 1901.

Holtman, Jack. *King of the High Missouri: The Saga of the Culbertsons.* Helena: Falcon Press, 1987.

Hubner, Brian. "'The Farwellians': Collected Biographical Information on Persons Associated with Farwell's Post, 1872-1873," ms., 1991. Fort Walsh National Historic Site, Maple Creek, Saskatchewan.

_____. "Horse Stealing and the Borderline: The NWMP and the Control of Indian Movement, 1874-1900." *Prairie Forum*, Vol. 20, No. 2 (Fall, 1995).

Hubner, Brian and Diane Payment. "Jean Louis Légaré," in *Dictionary of Canadian Biography*, Vol. 14. Toronto: University of Toronto Press, 1998.

Jacobsen, Hazel, comp. and ed. *Profile of Early Ovando, 1878-1900 (The Recollections of Wilda Lynn Mannix).* Deer Lodge, Montana: Platen Press, 1977.

Kehoe, Thomas F. *The Gull Lake Site: A Prehistoric Bison Drive Site in South Western Saskatchewan.* Publications in Anthropology and History, No. 1, Milwaukee Public Museum, 1973.

Kelson, Benjamin. "The Jews of Montana. Chapter I: Settlers in the Early Period, 1862-1885." *Western States Jewish Historical Quarterly,* 3, no. 3 (April 1971): 170-85.

Kennedy, Dan. *Recollections of an Assiniboine Chief.* Edited by J. R. Stevens. Toronto: McClelland and Stewart, 1972.

Kennedy, Margaret Anne. Personal communication, Dec. 7, 1989.

_____. "A Whiskey Trade Frontier on the Northwestern Plains." PhD diss., University of Calgary, 1991.

Kennedy, Margaret Anne and Brian O. K. Reeves, *An Inventory and Historical Description of Whiskey Posts in Southern Alberta*. 2 vols. Edmonton: Historic Sites Service, Alberta Culture ms., 1984.

Klassen, Henry C. "I. G. Baker and Company in Calgary, 1875-1884." *Montana: The Magazine of Western History*, 35 (Summer 1985): 40-54.

_____. "International Enterprise: The House of T. C. Power & Bro. in the Cypress Hills Trade, 1875-1893." *Saskatchewan History*, 43 (Spring 1991): 57-71.

Klein, Alan Michael. "Adaptive Strategies and Process on the Plains: The 19th Century Cultural Sink." PhD Diss., Buffalo: State University of New York, 1977.

Kurz, Rudolph Friederich. *Journal of Rudolph Friederich Kurz*, Smithsonian Institution, Bureau of American Ethnology, Bulletin 115, ed. J. N. B. Hewitt. Washington: US Government Printing Office, 1937.

Lande, George. Personal communication, July 9, 1990. Pryor, Montana.

_____. Taped interview, April 10, 1991. Pryor, Montana.

Larpenteur, Charles. *Forty Years a Fur Trader*, Vol. I, New York: Francis P. Harper, 1898.

Leacock, Eleanor Burke. "Montagnais Women and the Jesuit Program for Colonization." In *Rethinking Canada: The Promise of Women's History.* Edited by Veronica Strong-Boag and Anita Clair Fellman. Toronto: Copp Clarke Pitman, 1986.

Lee, David. "Foremost Man and His Band." *Saskatchewan History*, 36, no. 3 (Autumn 1983): 94-101.

Leveillie, Gabriel. "Transcript of Tape Recording made by Gabriel (Gab) Leveillie at Maple Creek Detachment, Feb. 14, 1957. Interviewed by Inspector T. E. Mudiman, O/C Swift Current Sub-Division." Medicine Hat, Alberta: Medicine Hat Museum and Art Gallery Archives.

Limmerick, Patricia Nelson. *The Legacy of Conquest. The Unbroken Past of the American West.* New York: W. W. Norton & Co., 1987.

McCloy, T. R. ". . . the descendants of John McKay and Mary Favell . . .," ms., 1983 ed. Medicine Hat, Alberta: Medicine Hat Museum and Art Gallery Archives.

_____. Personal communication, Oct. 24, 1989, and July 10, 1990. Calgary, Alberta.

McCullough, A. B. Papers Relating to the North-West Mounted Police and Fort Walsh. Manuscript Report No. 213. Ottawa: Parks Canada, Department of Indian and Native Affairs, 1977.

McDougall, John. *On Western Trails in the Early Seventies: Frontier Life in the Canadian North-West.* Toronto: W. Biggs, 1911.

MacEwan, Grant. "Sitting Bull." *Dictionary of Canadian Biography*, Vol. ii. Toronto: University of Toronto Press, 1998, p. 870.

McKay, W. Henry. "The Story of Edward McKay." *Canadian Cattlemen* 10, no. 2 (Sept. 1947): 76-77, 100-01 and 105.

McKenzie, N. M. W. J. "The Men of the Hudson's Bay Company," Fort William, ON: *Times-Journal Press*, 1921, pp. 70-71.

McLeod, C. H. Papers. University of Montana Archives, Missoula, Montana.

McLeod, Ellen. *Fort Walsh, Saskatchewan*. National Historic Sites Service, Manuscript Report No. 62. Ottawa: National and Historic Parks Branch, 1969.

Milloy, John S. *The Plains Cree: Trade, Diplomacy and War, 1790-1870*. Manitoba Studies in Native History IV. Winnipeg: The University of Manitoba Press, 1988.

Miller, David. *Encyclopedia of North American Indians: Native American History, Culture and Life from Paleo-Indians to the Present*, Frederick Hoxie (Ed.); Boston and New York: Houghton, Mifflin, 1996.

Morgan, Edwin Charles. *North-West Mounted Police, 1873-1883*. National Historic Parks and Sites Branch, Manuscript Report No. 113. Ottawa: Parks Canada, 1970.

Morgan, Dale L. and Eleanor Towles Harris (Eds.). "The biography of Etienne Provost." In *The Rocky Mountain Journals of William Marshall Anderson: The West in 1834*. San Marino: The Huntington Library, 1967.

Morice, Adrian Gabriel. *Dictionnaire historique des Canadiens et des Métis français de l'ouest*. Québec: J. P. Garneau, 1908.

Morris, Alexander. *The Treaties of Canada with the Indians of Manitoba and the Northwest Territories, Including the Negotiations on Which They Were Based, and Other Information Relating Thereto*. Toronto: Willing and Williamson, 1880.

Overholser, Joel. *Fort Benton: World's Innermost Port*. Fort Benton: Joel Overholser, 1987.

_____. Letter, Aug. 25, 1983, "Life in Whoop-Up Country" file. Maple Creek, Saskatchewan: Fort Walsh National Historic Site Library.

_____. Personal communications: Sept. 26, 1989; Nov. 3, 1989; Dec. 14, 1989; June 25, 1991; Sept. 26, 1991. Fort Benton, Montana.

Perry, Richard. "The Fur Trade and the Status of Women in the Western Subartic." *Ethnohistory*, 26, no. 4 (Fall 1979): 363-75.

Peterson, Jacqueline. "Many Roads to Red River: Métis Genesis in the Great Lakes Region." In *The New Peoples: Being and Becoming Métis in North America,* edited by Jacqueline Peterson and Jennifer S. H. Brown. Manitoba Studies in Native History I. Winnipeg: University of Manitoba Press, 1985.

Phillips, Paul C. "The Fur Trade in Montana." *The Montana Past: An Anthology.* Edited by Michael P. Malone and Richard B. Roeder. Missoula: University of Montana Press, 1969.

Power, Thomas C. Papers. Helena, Montana Montana Historical Society.

Prucha, Francis Paul. *Indian Policy in the United States: Historical Essays.* Lincoln: University of Nebraska Press, 1981.

Racette, Sherry Farrell. "Sewing ourselves together: Clothing, decorative arts and the expression of Métis and half breed identity," PhD Diss. University of Manitoba, 2004.

Ray, Arthur. *Indians in the Fur Trade: Their Role as Hunters, Trappers and Middlemen in the Lands southwest of Hudson's Bay, 1660-1870.* Toronto: University of Toronto Press, 1974.

Report of the Royal Commission on Aboriginal Peoples. "Restructuring the Relationship" section on "Treaties" Ottawa: Canada Communication Group, 1996.

Rich, E. E. *The Fur Trade and the Northwest to 1857.* Toronto: McClelland and Stewart, 1967.

Rondeau, Clovis. *La Montagne de Bois (Willow Bunch, Sask.): Histoire de la Saskatchewan meridionale.* Québec: L'Action Sociale, 1923.

Rowe, Charles. "The Bluff of Fred Kanouse." *Rowe Family History,* n.d., pp. 80-83.

Saindon, Bob, and Bunky Sullivan. "Taming the Missouri and Treating the Depression: Fort Peck Dam." *Montana: The Magazine of Western History,* 27, No. 3 (July 1977).

Saum, Lewis O. "From Vermont to Whoop-Up Country: Some Letters of D. W. Davis." *Montana: The Magazine of Western History,* 35 (Summer 1985): 56-71.

Savage, Candace. "Eight Thousand Years Down." *Canadian Geographic* (Vol. 126, no. 6), Dec. 2006.

Sealy, D. B. "Jerry Potts." *Dictionary of Canadian Biography,* Vol. 12. Toronto: University of Toronto Press, 1990.

Sharp, Paul F. *Merchant Princes of the Plains.* Montana Heritage Series No. 5. Helena: Montana Historical Society Press, 1955.

_____. *Whoop-Up Country: The Canadian-American West, 1865-1885.* Minneapolis: University of Minnesota Press, 1955.

Sprague, D. N. and R. R. Fry (Comps.). *The Genealogy of the First Métis Nation: The Development and Dispersal of the Red River Settlement.* Winnipeg: Pemmican Publications, 1983.

Spry, Irene. "The Transition from a Nomadic to a Settled Economy in Western Canada, 1856-96." *Transactions of the Royal Society of Canada,* 4th series, Vol. 6 (1968): 203-29.

Steele, Samuel B. *Forty Years in Canada.* New York: Dodd, Mead and Company, 1915.

Stegner, Wallace E. *Wolf Willow; a History, a Story, and a Memory of the Last Plains Frontier.* Toronto: Macmillan of Canada, 1955.

Stevens, Isaac Ingalls. *Report of Exploration of a Route for the Pacific Railroad, near the Forty-seventh and Forty-ninth Parallels, from St. Paul to Puget Sound.* Washington: n.p., 1855.

Sunder, John E. *The Fur Trade on the Upper Missouri, 1840-1865.* Norman: University of Oklahoma Press, 1965.

Tharpp, Dan L. *Encyclopedia of Frontier Biography.* 3 vols. Glendale: A. H. Clark, 1988.

Tobias, John. "Canada's Subjugation of the Plains Cree, 1879-1885." *Canadian Historical Review*, 64, Dec. 1983.

_____. "Protection, Civilization, Assimilation: An Outline History of Canada's Indian Policy" in J. R. Miller (Ed.) *Sweet Promises.* Toronto: University of Toronto Press, 1991.

Treaty 7 Tribal Council and Elders with Walter Hildebrandt, Dorothy First Rider, and Sarah Carter. *The True Spirit and Original Intent of Treaty 7.* Montreal: McGill-Queen's University Press, 1996.

Turner, Frederick. *Beyond Geography.* New York: Viking, 1980.

Turner, John Peter. *The North-West Mounted Police 1873-1893.* 2 vols. Ottawa: King's Printer, 1950.

US Census, 1870. Montana.

Utley, Robert M. *The Indian Frontier of the American West, 1846-1890.* Albuquerque: University of New Mexico Press, 1984.

_____. *The Lance and the Shield.* New York: Henry Holt, 1993.

Van Kirk, Sylvia. *Many Tender Ties: Women in Fur Trade Society in Western Canada 1670-1870.* Winnipeg: Watson and Dwyer, 1980.

Waiser, William A. "The North-West Mounted Police in 1874-1889: A Statistical Study," Research Bulletin No. 117. Ottawa: Parks Canada, 1979.

Weeks, Mary L. *The Last Buffalo Hunter. As told to her by Norbert Welsh.* New York: Thomas Nelson & Sons, 1939.

Williams, Glyndwr. "The Hudson's Bay Company and the Fur Trade: 1670-1870." *The Beaver*, special ed., Autumn 1983, rpt. 1991.

Wilson, A. (Ed). *The Letters of Charles John Brydges, 1879-82.* Winnipeg: Hudson's Bay Record Society, 1979.

Wood, Jim, personal communication, Aug. 9, 1992. Loma, Montana.

Allen to Galt, June 27, 1881 in PAC, RG 10, Vol. 4325.

I. G. Baker Co. to Galt, Feb. 14, 1882 in PAC, RG 10, Vol. 3744, file 295-06-3.

C. Denny to E. Dewdney, Jan. 9, 1882 in PAC, RG 10, Vol. 3744, file 295-06-2.

Denny to Dewdney, Nov. 20, 1881 in PAC, RG 10, Vol. 3744, file 295-06-1.

Denny to Dewdney, Nov. 9, 1881 in PAC, RG 10, Vol. 3744, file 295-06-1.

Department of Indian Affairs to Dewdney, May 11, 1882.

Dewdney to S.G.I.A., Jan. 1, 1882 in *C. P. Sessional Papers* (1882) Vol. 15, no. 6, pp. 37–45, 54–59.

Dewdney to S.G.I.A., Jan. 2, 1880 in *C. P. Sessional Papers* (1880) Vol. 3, no. 4, pp. 76–79.

Dewdney to Irvine, Oct. 27, 1882 in PAC, RG 10, Vol. 3744, file 295-06-2.

Dewdney to McDonald, May 25, 1883 in PAC, RG 10, Vol. 3744, file 295-06-3.

Dewdney to Macdonald, Oct. 24, 1883 in PAC, RG 10, Vol. 3744, file 295-06-3.

Edwards to McDonald, May 13, 1884 in PAC, RG 10, Vol. 3744, file 295-06-3.

Edwards to McDonald, May 13, 1884 in PAC, RG 10, Vol. 3745, file 295-06-1.

Edwards to McDonald, May 20, 1884 in PAC, RG 10, Vol. 3744, file 295-06-3.

Galt to Dewdney, July 18, 1881 in PAC, RG 10, Vol. 3744, file 295-06-1.

Galt to McDonald, June 20, 1882 in PAC, RG 10, Vol. 3744, file 295-06-2.

Galt to Macdonald, May 24, 1881 in PAC, RG 10, Vol. 3744, file 295-06-1.

Galt to Vankoughnet, May 18, 1882 in PAC, RG 10, Vol. 3744, file 295-06-2.

Hourie to McDonald, Oct. 18, 1882 in PAC, RG 10, Vol. 3744, file 295-06-2.

Irvine to White, May 30, 1882 in PAC, RG 10, Vol. 3744, file 295-06-2.

Jukes to White (Jukes Report), Oct. 17, 1882 in PAC, RG 10, Vol. 3744, file 295-06-3.

John A. Macdonald, Minister Interior to Governor General, June 30, 1879 in *C .P. Sessional Papers* (1878) Vol. 8, no. 10, pp. xxxi–xxxiv.

McDonald to Galt, Aug. 1, 1882 in PAC, RG 10, Vol. 3744, file 295-06-2.

McDonald to Galt, July 29, 1882 in PAC, RG 10, Vol. 3744, file 295-06-2.

McDonald to Galt, July 31, 1882 in PAC, RG 10, Vol. 3744, file 295-06-2.

McDonald to Dewdney, Nov. 11, 1882 in PAC, RG 10, Vol. 3744, file 295-06-3.

McIllree to Dewdney Feb. 15, 1882 in PAC, RG 10, Vol. 3744, file 295-06-2.

McIllree to Dewdney, Dec. 2, 1882 in PAC, RG 10, Vol. 3744, file 295-06-3.

Nelson to Dewdney, Dec. 5, 1885 in *C. P. Sessional Papers* (1886) Vol. no. 4, pp. 146–151.

Nelson to S.G.I.A., Dec. 29, 1882 in *C. P. Sessional Papers* (1883) Vol. 4, no. 5, pp. 214–215.

Norman to Dewdney, Dec. 27, 1882 in PAC, RG 10, Vol. 3744, file 295-06-3.

Patrick to Dewdney, Dec. 16, 1880 in PAC, RG 10, Vol. 3730, file 26219.

S.G.I.A. to Governor General, Dec. 31, 1881 in *C. P. Sessional Papers* (1882) Vol. 5, no. 6, pp. vii–ix, xxxi–xxxii.

Vankoughnet to John A. Macdonald, Oct. 10, 1881 in PAC, RG 10, Vol. 3744, file 295-06-1.

Wadsworth to Dewdney, July 3, 1880 in PAC, RG 10, Vol. 3744, file 295-06-01.

Wadsworth to Vankoughnet, Aug. 29, 1881 in PAC, RG 10, Vol. 3744, file 295-06-1.

NEWSPAPERS

Fort Benton Record, Fort Benton, Montana.

Helena (Daily/Weekly) Herald, Helena, Montana.

Helena Daily Independent, Helena, Montana.

Kendall Miner, Kendall, Montana.

Medicine Hat Daily News, Medicine Hat, Alberta.

River Press (Daily/Weekly), Fort Benton, Montana.

Winnipeg Standard, Winnipeg, Manitoba.

INDEX

Blackfoot 20, 25, 33, 44, 55, 123, 131; alliance with Cree 33; and Big Bear 143-4; and buffalo wars 33, 44; and trade 32, 41, 47; and US government 46; and violence 49; arrival on plains 19-20, 25; as danger in Hills 42; as enemies of the Cree and Nakoda 33-4, 45, 90, 94; as enemies of Dakota 103; holy women 28; social structure of 21, 33; traditional territory 18, 21

Blair Athol 149

Blonde Hair (Pahazzi) 64. *See* Hammond, George

Blood 20, 32, 40, 55, 68, 69, 87, 104

Bozeman Trail 100

Bray, John Henry Grisham 51

Breland, Mary 149

Brydges, Charles John 83, 85

buffalo 17, 19, 42, 104, 120, 121, 148; and prairie fires 114; depletion of the herds 29, 30, 31, 32, 33-4, 39, 41-2, 55, 83, 89, 90, 93, 95, 113, 143; hunting 12, 20, 24-9, 32, 68, 74, 102, 125, 132; trade in hides 36, 38-9, 5156, 59, 68-9, 106

Buffalo Bill's Wild West Show 117

"Buffalo Wars" 33, 44

Calling River People 94

Carry the Kettle *27*, 137

Cheyenne 100-2, 106

Cheyenne River 67, 106

Christie, W. J. 97

Civil War 12, 38, 46, 49-50, 69, 70

Close Kill 70

Confederation 32

Conrad, Charles 47, 50

Conrad, William 47, 50, 51

Cook, Caroline 50

Coombs, Glorianna 62

Coombs, Sarah 62

Cowesses 95, 107, 142

Cowie, Isaac 13, 41, 48, 61, 121; and trading post 44-5, 50

Crazy Horse 101-2, 105

Cree: alliance with Nakoda 33-4; alliance with Blackfoot 33; and Big Bear 143-4; and buffalo wars 33, 44; and changing economies 27, 40, 96, 132; and Cypress Hills Massacre 59; and decline of buffalo herds 33, 70-1, 104; and Ottawa 89, 141; and reserves in Cypress Hills 144-5; and trade 51; and violence 49; as danger in the Hills 42; as fur trade provisioners 32; as middlemen in the fur trade 31, 32, 33; cycles of movement 21, 90-1; dependence on trade 32; enemies of Dakota 31, 104, 108; independent of reserves 143, 144-5; social structure of 21, 33, 89, 141; starvation 141, 143-4; traditional territory 20-1, 31

Crook, George 101, 102

Crooked Arm 61, 107

Crooked Lake 130, 139

Crow 20, 33, 51, 104

Crow's Dance 107

Crozier, Supt L. N. F. 115, 116, 117

Culbertson, Alexander 50, 67

Cullen, W. E. 74

Curly (Crow scout) 102

Custer, Lt. Col. George Armstrong 98, 100-2

Cypress Hills Massacre 13, 51, 57, 59, 69-73, 74-5, 76, 78, 120, 123, 150

Cypress Hills: as spiritual place 12, 120, 121, 125; climate of 15, 39, 95, 128; geological history of 12, 14-15; vegetation of 12, 14, 157; wildlife in 15-16, 18, 143

Cypress Lake 144

Dakota 20, 63; and Nez Percé 99; and Sitting Bull in Canada 102, 106-10; and starvation 101, 103, 106, 114-5, 116, 117; and the War of 1812 99, 107; traditional territory of 99, 104; US missions for return of 106, 108, 110-17. *See also* Little Big Horn, Battle of

Daniels (Métis scout) 106

Day Star (Kisecawchuck) 94

De Courby, Fr. Jules 43

Denig, Edwin 67, 121

Dewdney, Edgar 124, 126-8, 129-31, 134, 135-6, 144

Diehl, Charles 111

Downstream people 94-5, 97

Dumont, Gabriel 117

Durfee and Peck 46, 60, 61

Duval, John C. 69

provisioners for the fur trade 44; cycles of movement 40, 42, 43; discontent 41, 98; in US military custody ; leaving the Hills 42; scouts 74, 102, 106, 110; seeking treaty 118; settlements 41

Miles, Gen Nelson A. 109, 115

military force, American use of 61, 67, 98-9, 101-2

Milk River 41, 42, 43, 49, 61, 102

Milloy, John 33

Mills, David, Minister of the Interior, 140

Minnesota Massacres 103, 109

missionaries 77, 91, 95, 99, 115, 120

Missouri River 42, 46, 60

Morin, Joseph "Blackbird" 105, 106, 110

Morris, Alexander 96-7, 139

Murphy, Neel, and Co. 46

Musselshell River 63, 109

Nakoda: alliance with Cree 33, 120; and decline of the buffalo 27, 104, 121; and Home Farm Plan 125, 127-8; and Ottawa 89, 129; and Sweet Grass Massacre 49; and the Cypress Hills Massacre 59, 69-74, 120, 123; and trade 51, 120; and trapping 142; and Treaty 4 98, 122-4, 128; and violence 70 ; arrival on plains 19, 25; as middlemen in fur trade 32; independent of reserves 143; Indian Head Reserve 131-3, 136-7; origin of name 119; removal from Cypress Hills 129-132; reserves in Cypress Hills 124-5, 130-31, 132; social structure 120; starvation 120, 129; tensions with Moses Solomon 69-70; traditional territory 119-20; victims of prejudice 74

National Policy 32, 89, 140

Nekaneet *141*, 144-5

Nez Percé 43, 51, 99, 109-10, 114, 123

North West Company (NWC) 32, 55

Northwestern Fur Company (NWFC) 46, 47

North-West Mounted Police (NWMP) 12, 74, 85, 87, 98, 118, 140, 150; and Dakota 105-7 109, 110; at Fort Walsh 78-82, 83, 88; and move to Maple Creek 83, 86, 144, 145; and rations 56, 86, 114; and the March West 76-8, 83; and trade 83-5, 86, 89; and US military 104-5, 115 ; arrival of 22, *27*, 37, 51, 57

Oetelaar, Gerald A. 17-18, *18, 19*

Oglaḷa 101

O'Hanlon, Thomas 61

O'Hare, Peter 51

Okanese 97

Old Wives Lake 94

Oldman River 38, 69

O'Soup, Louis 95

Ottawa 89, 95-6, 139-40; and Aboriginal policy 140-1; and Dakota 108; and government contracts 74, and Nakoda 129; on Cypress Hills Massacre 74

Ouilette, Antoine 110

Oxarart Ranch 149

Pahazzi (Blonde Hair) 64. See Hammond, George

Parsonage, Everett 148

Pasquah 95

Peace River 42

Peepeekis 95

Piegan, 20, 32, 51, 55, 67, 104

pemmican, as a staple 24, 30, 90-1; trade in 12, 21, 27, 39-40, 41, 44, 48

Perry, Richard 36

Peterson, Andrew 68

Piapot 27, 95, 97, 142, 143; at Indian Head 132, 133-4, 137

Piapot Creek 148-9

Pinto Horse Butte 80

Plains Cree 25, 33, 104. See Cree

Plains Peoples 20, 40; and agriculture 20, 31, 89, 95, 97-8; and Ottawa 89, 95-6; and starvation 95; and violence 43-4; and war 48; cultural differences with Europeans 31, 35-6, 90-4; cycles of movement 21, 40, 90; dependence on buffalo 27; European view of 90, 91-2; southern influences on 20

Plains Ojibwe 20. See Saulteaux

Poor Man. See Kawacatoose

Porcupine Creek 43

Potts, Jerry 50, 78

poundmaker 28-9

Powder River 101

Power, Thomas 46, 47

prehistoric mammals 16

prehistoric peoples in the Hills 14, 16-18, 24-5

THE AUTHORS

HISTORIAN AND POET WALTER HILDEBRANDT was born in Brooks, Alberta, and now lives in Edmonton. He has worked as an historian for Parks Canada and as a consultant to the Treaty 7 Tribal Council, the Federation of Saskatchewan Indian Nations, and the Banff Bow Valley Task Force. He is co-author of the *True Spirit and Original Intent of Treaty 7*, and author of *Views from Battleford: Constructed Visions of an Anglo-Canadian West*. He has published four books of poetry, including *Sightings,* nominated in 1992 for the McNally-Robinson Book of the Year for Manitoba. His book, *Where the Land Gets Broken*, largely about the Cypress Hills, won the Stephan G. Stephansson Award for poetry in Alberta for 2005.

BRIAN HUBNER, born in Regina, Saskatchewan, is currently an archivist with the University of Manitoba Archives & Special Collections, and was previously employed at the Archives of Manitoba, Queen's University Archives, Kingston, and at the Library and Archives of Canada in Ottawa. He has a Master of Arts (history, in archival studies) from the University of Manitoba, and a Master of Arts (history), from the University of Saskatchewan. Brian has delivered conference papers and published articles on subjects related to Canadian Aboriginal peoples, including "Horse Stealing and the Borderline: The N.W.M.P. and the Control of Indian Movement, 1874-1900." His most recent publication is, "'This is the Whiteman's Law': Aboriginal Resistance, Bureaucratic Change, and the Census of Canada, 1830-2006." Brian lives in Winnipeg and is married with two children.